Hillary Rodham Clinton

What Every American Should Know

Christian Josi

Executive Director
American Conservative Union

American Conservative Union
Alexandria, VA

Mail Orders: 800-426-1357
E-mail: 72557.3635@compuserve.com (for orders)
                www.conservative.org (to ACU)

The American Conservative Union
1007 Cameron Street
Alexandria, VA 22314
703-836-8602

Printed in the United States of America.

5   4   3   2   1   /   01   00

Contents

Preface

The "real" Hillary Rodham Clinton, with her many faces, is a terribly complex individual—much more so than either her sycophants or her worst enemies believe. If, like a jigsaw puzzle, you could piece together her life, it would still be virtually impossible to arrive at a clear and unambiguous portrait. So this book is by no means an attempt at a psychological profile. There are plenty of those floating around these days, from both hostile and sympathetic observers; and, according to reports, there are many more to come.

In fact, it's in response to the current bull market on "Hillary books" that I set out to write this one. My aim is to give to the average reader and voter—who would likely never have the time or the resources to acquire and comb through these many works—an abbreviated yet clear snapshot of the words, deeds, and misdeeds of the most self-absorbed and power-struck First Lady in our nation's history. This book is by no means a chronicle of Clinton scandals—Lord knows that would take more space than I've been allotted here—but it is a summary of those scandals that seem to have come about primarily as a result of Hillary's ego and actions. Many, I believe, will find such a summary useful as the First Lady steps out in force from the shadow of her husband. With her eyes fixed on a bid for the United States Senate, or perhaps even higher office, I believe that the information herein should be read and understood by the largest possible audience—and fast.

With that end in mind, I want to state that this is a highly derivative work. I'm fortunate to have the benefit of many years' worth of research and toil by distinguished authors, columnists and researchers, the best of which I have tried to harvest and carefully document. The result is a brief compendium of what I believe are the "must knows" about Hillary and her world. The sources and publications cited throughout this book are, in my view, the most accurate available. If the reader is so inclined, I highly recommend seeking out these sources to learn more about the issues raised and to acquire more information about Hillary the person, the wife and mother, the First Lady, and the political animal.

I would like to thank the one million members of the American Conservative Union, the nation's oldest and largest conservative grassroots organization, for their steadfast support of our work. And to my friends back home in the New York State Conservative Party, I owe deep gratitude for the inspiration and education I received during my political years there.

Introduction

More books have been written about Bill and Hillary Clinton than most people will ever read. There are books about their lives, their psychology, their marriage and their single-minded pursuit of power. There are books about Whitewater and Monica, about how they've squandered public trust, and about their ambition. Some break new ground and some are barely readable. So the question you must ask as you open this one is simple enough: Why do I need to read yet another book about these people, or about Hillary?

The answer to that question is just as simple. You have to read it because it draws together the facts that should make anyone question the first lady's political motives and goals. Hillary Rodham Clinton isn't going to go away. She is intent upon seeking the power to tell the rest of us how we ought to live our lives and seeks power so she can force her views on us whether we like them or not.

But to do that she must submit her views and her record to the public for approval. She has chosen to do this in New York and it is my firm belief that anyone who is in a position to vote for or against her in New York ought to know just who this woman is, what she really wants, and what she's done. This book may not break new ground, but it does answer those questions.

In compiling the facts about a very public woman, Christian Josi has performed a signal public service and it is my hope that every New Yorker will read what he has written. In this new book, Josi, who is himself a New Yorker and serves as my Executive Director at the American Conservative Union, presents a disturbing portrait of Hillary Rodham Clinton.

The facts lead the reader to the conclusion that her quest for the seat in the United States Senate being vacated by Daniel Patrick Moynihan may be just a step in her drive for power. Josi believes, in fact, that her goal is not the Senate, but the Oval Office now occupied by her husband.

Hillary Clinton is herein regarded as a political Machiavellian of the first order whose decision to "stand by her man" during the Monica Lewinsky scandal may well have been motivated far more by her future political ambitions than any remaining loyalty to her husband.

Bill Clinton's administration will, in my opinion, go down as one of the most corrupt in U.S. history. The damage done as a result of the many ethical lapses, scandals, and overall wanton disregard for the safety and security of our nation will become increasingly clear as the years pass. Interestingly, an objective view of the record reveals that the primary force behind much of this scandal and damage was, with very few exceptions, Hillary rather than Bill. It was she who insisted on staffing the White House with ideologues, pushing a health care plan that would have put virtually all important medical decisions in the hands of government bureaucrats. And it was she who unleashed the might of America's military on the civilian population of the Balkans. The Whitewater records point to Hillary and it is her fingerprints one finds on virtually every questionable activity launched since her husband took office.

This book, the first by young ACU Executive Director Christian Josi, sheds light on the real Hillary Clinton—her arrogance, her lust for power and money, her ties to the radical Left in years past, and the far-left vision that she would impose on America today that fuels her drive for high office.

ACU aims to put a copy of this eye-opening book in the hands of every voter in New York State. ACU launched this project because the New York media (which is overwhelmingly liberal) appears determined to do all it can to let bygones be bygones as far as Hillary is concerned. She has yet to face a tough press grilling and has been allowed to get away with far more than most candidates. Her press conferences resemble cheerleading sessions, with some reporters acting as the lead cheerleaders.

She is scarcely ever asked any tough questions about the central role she played in the majority of the 38 separate scandals (at the latest count) that have engulfed the Clinton Administration. The facts reveal that the first lady is a key figure in "Chinagate," "Filegate," "Travelgate," "Hillarycare," "Cattlegate," Whitewater, the ransacking of Vince Foster's White House office after his death, the magical reappearance of her law firm billing records (which had been subpoenaed two years earlier), and the Webster Hubbell "money-for-silence" scandal, among others. Any one of these scandals would endanger if not destroy a normal Senate candidacy. This woman, who now wants the people of her newly-adopted state to send her to the U.S. Senate, masterminded the selling of seats on official U.S. trade missions to "Fat Cat" Democrat contributors (starting at $50,000 a seat) and treated the historic Lincoln Bedroom as a Clinton Bed & Breakfast for contributors to the 1996 Clinton-Gore reelection effort.

A hallmark of her latest campaign is her total disregard for the taxpayers' money. She has used Air Force planes (at taxpayer expense) to ferry her around the state, used White House staff (again at taxpayer expense) to create her campaign web site and perform other campaign-related duties. If any of us acted in this manner federal election officials and prosecutors would be all over us.

This book should prompt readers to ask: Does Hillary Clinton possess the common sense or integrity we seek in our elected representatives? Does she really want to represent New York? And is Hillary running for Senate primarily because she loves New York and just wants to do what's best for the state, or does she have much grander ambitions for herself in mind?

We at the ACU have decided to do all we can to see to it that as many New Yorkers as possible see (and read) this book before next November because we are convinced that an informed electorate is vital to a working democracy. The issues facing us are too important to be turned over to people who put their own political and personal ambitions above those of the nation. Every New York voter will decide whether Hillary Clinton is the sort of person he or she wants in the Senate, but that decision should be informed by a full review of the facts rather than a glance at a 30-second television spot. If we have anything to say about it, every New Yorker will have those facts and Christian's book is a valuable first step in this important effort. Now all we have to do is print and distribute enough copies to create the informed electorate America's founders knew we all could trust.

The American Conservative Union is this nation's largest conservative grassroots advocacy organization. It was founded in 1964 and today we have more than a million members throughout the country. As ACU's Chairman, I not only endorse Christian's book, but pledge that none of us will rest until the truth about Hillary is available to every New Yorker.

I sincerely hope that after reading Christian's book, you will join ACU's effort to make sure every voter in New York State has a full picture of exactly who Hillary Rodham Clinton is before deciding who will represent New York State in the United States Senate.

Use the order form at the back of this book to order additional copies of **Hillary Rodham Clinton** to give to your friends. Please also take this opportunity to send whatever contribution you possibly can to ACU to help fund this much-needed VOTER ALERT effort.

David Keene, Chairman
THE AMERICAN CONSERVATIVE UNION
America's conservative voice since 1964

A former newspaper editor who had lunch with Hillary while she was First Lady of Arkansas reported the following exchange: "During a lapse in a conversation about what Bill wanted to do, I asked her, 'What do you want to do?' She leaned toward me, eyes ablaze, and said in as intense a voice as I ever heard, 'I want to run something!'"[1]

"There are some things we feel, feelings that our prevailing acquisitive and competitive corporate life, including tragically the universities, is not the way of life for us."[2]

"It's a real honor for me to be ever compared to Eleanor Roosevelt."[3]

"Certain myths ... serve only to inhibit the development of a realistic family policy in this country: the myth of the housewife whose life centers only on her home and ... the myth, or perhaps more accurately, the prejudice, that each family should be self-sufficient."[4]

PART I

The Early Years

*"Every protest, every dissent ...is unabashedly an attempt to
forge an identity in this particular age. That attempt at forging
for many of us over the past four years has meant coming to
terms with our humanness."[5]*

*"Decisions about motherhood and abortion, schooling, cosmetic
surgery, treatment of venereal disease, or employment, and others
where the decision or lack of one will affect the child's future
should not be made unilaterally by parents."[6]*

CHAPTER I

Who Is Hillary Rodham Clinton?

Though it's true, as I said in the Preface, that the private Hillary
Rodham Clinton is an enigma, it's not particularly difficult
to understand the public woman. We've seen and read varying
depictions of this Hillary—the student protester; the defender of
the Black Panthers; the advocate of "children's rights" as defined
by radicals; the Watergate prosecutor; the teeth-grinding feminist;
the First Lady; the possible senatorial candidate; the rumored

presidential aspirant; and, above all, the militant control freak. In these roles, she's a textbook case—a woman radicalized by the Sixties, who believes American society, with its tainted history, is an inherently evil thing that must be transformed by any means necessary—for its own good, of course. However, the contradictory facts of her life pose interesting questions. For instance:

- Why would Hillary, the young feminist with a fancy for the liberal salons, marry Bill Clinton—Hot Springs' favorite Bubba—and choose to live in his dark and backward Arkansas world?
- Why has she tolerated his continued and obsessive adulteries, so flagrant and numerous they have caused porn-peddler Larry Flynt to profess admiration?
- How could a woman who blames Wall Street and corporate greed for the ills of the nation justify becoming a trader in cattle futures—and, according to reputable analysts, a crooked trader at that?
- How could a liberal Democrat activist who professes to be a champion of the little people scornfully step on and squash so many of them in her rise to power and prominence?
- All in all, why would someone who seeks to be regarded as "pure in principle" toss aside principles so often in favor of political advantage?

In order to understand the public Hillary Clinton better, a brief primer on Hillary Rodham is in order to shed light on who she is and where she—and her husband—came from.

The Rodhams were conventional middle-class suburbanites who lived northwest of Chicago. They were comfortable but neither rich nor socially prominent. Hillary's father, Hugh Rodham, started a small custom-drapery business after World War II; and eventually he was successful enough to afford a house in Park Ridge, a community composed largely of the more-affluent blue collar workers and the less-affluent white collar workers.

Some biographers have suggested that Park Ridge was (and is) an exclusive suburb inhabited by the most privileged. Christopher Andersen, in his absorbing book *Bill and Hillary: The Marriage,* describes the community as "leafy, prosperous, Republican-to-the-core...."[7] While this description is not entirely inaccurate, it's certainly misleading.

Park Ridgers weren't quite so well off as Andersen paints them. The suburb may have been the mecca of successful foremen and plumbers, but it was no more than a holding pen for young Yuppie couples, who focused their ultimate dreams on the more fashionable communities of Kenilworth and Winnetka, off to the north. (Which were very similar in profile to the Clintons' new adopted community of Chappaqua, New York.)

However, Park Ridge was a secure, orderly, and respectable place in which to grow up. The Rodham family was, overall, firmly established in the middle class, a status unlike that of "Dude," Virginia, and young Billy and Roger Clinton down in Hot Springs, Arkansas.

Hillary's mother, Dorothy Rodham, spent much of her life deferring to her husband and making home a happy place for her three children—Hillary, Hugh, Jr., and Tony.

However, because she felt intimidated by her husband, Dorothy went out of her way to nurture Hillary's ego, saying she was "determined that no daughter of mine was going to have to go through the agony of being afraid to say what she had on her mind. Just because she was a girl didn't mean she should be limited."[8]

One of the defining moments of Hillary's childhood came when she complained to her mother that a larger girl was bullying her. "There's no room in this house for cowards," Dorothy told her. "The next time she hits you, I want you to hit her back."[9]

Hillary came back victorious and ecstatic. The admiring neighborhood boys suddenly let her into their crowd. According to Dorothy, the "boys responded well to Hillary. She just took charge, and they let her."[10]

(It would become the story of her life—going after people she regarded as "bullies" and ordering the boys around.)

Andersen tells of another incident in which her mother gave Hillary a lesson in self-control:

> Dorothy pulled out a carpenter's level to teach her daughter
> how to maintain her emotional equilibrium. She held the level
> in front of Hillary, pointed to the bubble in the center, then
> tilted the level so that the bubble slid to one end and then to
> the other. "Imagine having the carpenter's level inside you,"
> she said. The trick, Dorothy told her daughter, was to remain
> calm, determined, focused, always in control—whatever it
> took "to keep the bubble in the center."[11]

(Hillary applied the lesson in most areas of her life; but after she met Bill Clinton, she gained a reputation for flinging horrendous temper fits, screaming obscenities, throwing objects, and lashing out at everyone around her. In most cases, these tantrums were connected in some way to his behavior.)

From the beginning, Hillary was extraordinarily bright and ambitious. She brought home excellent grades, participated in extracurricular activities, and was voted Most Likely to Succeed. However, when she became a teenager, she was no longer a hit with the boys—or many others it seems. In fact, the student newspaper once referred to her as "Sister Frigidaire."[12]

In later years, Dorothy Rodham would acknowledge that, with all the other lessons she had dispensed, she'd failed to give Hillary "advice on clothes and makeup and how to attract boys." While curiously silent on that subject, Dorothy was nonetheless "annoyed" by Hillary's drab appearance. "I used to think, 'Why can't she put on a little makeup?'"[13]

As for politics, Hugh Rodham was the family authority. Something of a curmudgeon—a petty tyrant in his own household and standoffish with his neighbors—he was regarded by many as an eccentric. He was a Taft Republican, and he chewed tobacco. So sure was he of his own views that he forced his children to watch the 1952 Republican National Convention, gavel-to-gavel, and forbade them to watch the Democratic counterpart.[14]

Dorothy—secretly in rebellion against her husband—was in fact a closet Democrat who voted for John F. Kennedy in 1960 and quietly tried to shape her daughter's political thinking. "How on earth," she would later boast, "do you think Hillary ever became a Democrat?"[15]

Perhaps not as the result of Dorothy Rodham's quiet advocacy.

In fact, while still in high school, Hillary became a "Goldwater Girl" and in 1964 campaigned for the Arizona senator in his unsuccessful bid for the presidency.[16]

However, other conflicting influences were at work, attempting to lay claim to her loyalty. In her early teens, she learned about the social gospel as a member of the First United Methodist Church. At 13, she and other teenagers were sent to baby-sit for minority migrant workers who were harvesting crops in Illinois. At 14, she was a member of the congregation's "University of Life," a group the Rev. Don Jones tirelessly indoctrinated with the simplistic and appealing dogmas of the Left.[17]

Jones showed them pictures of the victims of Franco's forces in the Spanish Civil War (no doubt, without mentioning comparable atrocities by the communists). And he took them to Chicago's south side to show them what he identified as the same conditions.

His point to the impressionable youngsters was obvious: America was no different from Franco's Spain.[18]

Jones also introduced Hillary and the rest of his political acolytes to Saul Alinsky, author of *Reveille for Radicals,* and to Martin Luther King, Jr., who delivered a lecture called "Sleeping Through the Revolution."[19] Despite this attempt to reshape her thinking, Hillary was still a Republican when she graduated from high school in 1965. However, as Hillary matured, Jones would become increasingly influential in her life.

The following fall, her parents drove her to Wellesley, then the most expensive women's college in the nation. There she registered for classes and was soon elected president of the Young Republicans.

Most young people—college students in particular—are like chameleons, taking on the protective coloration of the political and intellectual world around them. Hillary was no exception. Within a year, she had resigned as president of the Wellesley YRs and was beginning to involve herself in campus debates over civil rights, Vietnam, and capitalism. She wrote her senior thesis on the Johnson administration's Community Action Program, a product of the Great Society.[20]

From the Midwest rather than from the East, she was not born into that inner circle of wealth and status that has always dominated the Ivy League schools and the Seven Sisters. At Wellesley, she was an outsider who broke regional and class barriers—from managing to head a campus political organization while still a freshman, to becoming president of the student government at the beginning of her senior year, and, at the end, being chosen to give the student commencement address.

Her immediate and total success on campus can only be attributed to the strength of her will and the depth of her intelligence. Even at that age, she was a formidable woman who was well on her way to mastering the art of getting what she wanted.

Like so many undergraduates, Hillary quickly surrendered the values she'd brought to college and adopted the ones her professors and fellow students were promoting. She came to Wellesley the child of her father and left a child of the Sixties—a typical student of the times. She soon hated capitalism, thought American society was decadent, and yearned for drastic action to change the nation's misguided course.

Wellesley, like many Northeastern schools, had more than its share of Marxist faculty members. During that same period, an organizer for the Intercollegiate Studies Institute, a conservative youth group, reported that he found only five Wellesley students who were willing to come out of the closet and call themselves "conservatives." Even these complained of threats and harassment from both fellow students and faculty.[21]

All over the country, students were demonstrating against the war abroad and inequality at home, burning flags, staging sit-ins in the offices of terrified college presidents, and even torching and bombing buildings. While this orgiastic destruction was taking place, editorial writers and TV reporters were describing campus revolutionaries as "idealistic" and "peace-loving."

Hillary Rodham was not this kind of revolutionary. Perhaps she remembered the carpenter's level inside her. Perhaps her ambitions extended beyond Wellesley and the 1960s. Her mother had encouraged her to be the first woman on the U.S. Supreme Court. Riot and arson were not reliable avenues to the High Court or, for that matter, to the White House. Both goals were probably in the back of Hillary's mind. So while she shared the aims and ideology of student revolutionaries, she emerged as "a voice of reason" on the campus.

Yet these early years reflect an increasing commitment to leftist ideology:

- She brought Saul Alinsky to the Wellesley campus to give his views on revolution. So worshipful was she that Alinsky offered her a job after she graduated. She turned him down to continue her studies.[22]

- Her "University of Life" experiences now seemed important, and she carried on a correspondence with the Rev. Don Jones. Also she began to read a magazine for Methodist youth called *Motive,* which featured rhetorically titled articles such as "What would be so wrong about a Viet Nam run by Ho Chi Minh, a Cuba by Castro?"[23]

- *Motive* was edited by Carl Oglesby, described as a Marxist-Maoist, who—while Hillary was in college—was also president of Students for a Democratic Society (SDS). He advocated the use of violence to effect social change.[24]

- When black Senator Edward Brooke, in an address to Hillary's graduating class at Wellesley, attacked violence as a means of change, while expressing empathy for the goals of those who were rioting, student speaker Hillary Rodham stepped up to the podium and—in the imprecise and intemperate language students were using those days—told Brooke off: "Part of the problem with empathy with professed goals is that empathy doesn't do anything. We've had lots of empathy. We've had lots of sympathy, but we feel that for too long our leaders have used politics as the art of the possible. And the challenge now is to practice politics as the art of making what appears to be impossible, possible . . . We are, all of us, exploring a world that none of us understands and attempting to create within that uncertainly. But there are some things we feel, feelings that our prevailing, acquisitive, and competitive corporate life, including tragically the universities, is not the way of life for us."[25] It was the speech of a precocious brat, but it caught the attention of the Left nationwide.

After Wellesley, Hillary decided to study law at Yale; and as soon as she arrived, she threw herself into the anti-war movement, joining the League of Women Voters as a means of promoting leftist politics in the mainstream. She also involved herself in other student activities. Again, she immediately rose to the top.

- She was chosen to make the 50th anniversary speech to the League, and she took the podium wearing a black arm band commemorating the students killed at Kent State. Typical of student rhetoric at the time, her speech was shrill and Marxist in tone: "How much longer can we let corporations run us? Isn't it about time that they, as all the rest of our institutions, are held accountable to the people?"[26]

- In the spring of 1970, Black Panther leader Bobby Seale and seven fellow Panthers went on trial in New Haven for torturing and then murdering one of the brothers whom they suspected of squealing to the cops. Huey Newton and Jane Fonda came to town to lead protest rallies. After all, black radicals—particularly those dedicated to violent revolution—couldn't be expected to receive a fair trial from a corrupt WASP legal system. Hillary Rodham organized a group of students to monitor the trial for the American Civil Liberties Union. In the course of that trial, the police bombarded rowdy students with tear gas, and someone set fire to the law library. When the students planned their reaction, it was Hillary who presided over the meeting. One fellow student would later say that no one "could remember what the meeting was about—only that we were awed by her."

Yale students organized a strike in support of the Panthers, and Huey Newton termed the United States "fascist" and called for violent revolution. By then, such activities were familiar spectacles on almost every large campus nationwide. Spoiled, self-righteous middle-class students from Massachusetts to Texas were tearing down their own universities in the name of free speech and a classless society.[27]

- During her junior year, Hillary met Marian Wright Edelman and served as her summer intern in Washington. Edelman, a collectivist ideologue, was using "children's rights" as a weapon with which to advance her radical agenda, particularly to attack the institution of the family. As an intern, Hillary was assigned to Senator Walter Mondale's subcommittee on migrant labor, where she conducted interviews with workers in migrant labor camps, documenting the disgraceful conditions under which they worked.[28]

- At this stage, her righteous indignation against America and its capitalist system boiled over. When Minute Maid, a subdivision of Coca-Cola, was implicated in the migrant worker scandal, the CEO of Coca-Cola came to Washington to testify. An irate Hillary, forgetting the carpenter's level, confronted him at a congressional hearing and, shaking an accusing finger at him, said, "We're going to nail your ass! Nail your ass!"[29]

- Bobby Seale's lawyer introduced Hillary to Robert Treuhaft and his wife Jessica Mitford. Both were avowed communists, and Treuhaft for years served as the attorney for the Communist Party, USA. As the result of this meeting, Hillary spent the summer of 1971 as an intern in Treuhaft's law office in Berkeley.[30]

Few mainstream journalists have focused on this aspect of Hillary's intellectual development. Many dismiss her early activism as no more than the folly of youth—a natural expression of idealism in a time of social upheaval. ("What college student didn't go a little crazy in the Sixties?") Perhaps, as politically correct activists themselves, journalists see nothing worrisome about such a past. ("What's wrong with Saul Alinsky and Bob Treuhaft? Great

Americans.") And perhaps they don't want right-wingers to latch on to the issue—particularly now that Hillary threatens to become a major player on the national political stage.

One thing is certain: Unlike Sixties revolutionary Jerry Rubin (who became a stock broker), Hillary Rodham has never put the late Sixties and early Seventies behind her. Because she connected with so many leftist icons while she was in college and law school, she ended up as chairman of the Legal Services Corporation (LSC) and on the board of the Children's Defense Fund. Simply put, she never surrendered her Socialist leanings and commitment to the necessity of transforming lives through the magic of Big Government, as her health-care plan would later clearly illustrate.

But the injustices of capitalism and family life weren't the only things on her mind at Yale. By then, she'd met Bill Clinton and had fallen unpredictably, unequivocally in love.

Along Came Bill

Bill Clinton was a man like none Hillary Rodham had ever seen. Tall and trim, he looked like an athlete without having to be one. He was warm, outgoing, and exhibited the easy courtesy of a plantation heir, while professing the politics of a migrant worker. Good manners were *de rigueur* in Arkansas; radicalism was rarer.

Clinton had also learned a lesson that most men skip: He listened quietly and attentively when women talked, as if he really wanted to hear what they were saying. And there was a tender, thoughtful, disarming quality about him—one that made him all but irresistible.

He had something else women liked—a smooth self-confidence that bordered on cockiness, yet somehow stopped just short of the mark. He was never shy or awkward in their presence. He knew all the right moves and performed them flawlessly. Girls he'd seduced in high school remembered him as "sweet."

The manners, the tenderness, the warm grin, and the sunny dis-
position hit Hillary like a freight train. Here was a man who shared
her political agenda, yet wasn't an awkward left-wing geek who
made long coffee-house speeches about gender equality and treated
her like a housemaid.

Hillary thought she had "discovered" Bill Clinton—in fact, lit-
erally hundreds of meretricious cuties in Arkansas, Northern Virginia, England, and even New Haven had long ago discovered
him—in the backseats of cars, in motel rooms, and in scores of
less likely places. He'd been discovered so many times that he'd
probably lost count.

In fact, he had a real problem: He enjoyed "discovery" so much
that it had become a vocation with him. He was a serial seducer,
who, wherever he went, would bed as many women as he could
work into a busy schedule. It wasn't just something he *liked* to do.
It was something he *had* to do—an addiction, an obsession—the
only thing that overrode his almost boundless ambition.

Bill won a Rhodes Scholarship to Oxford, where his sex life continued to escalate. Andersen quotes a woman who knew him at the
time: "There were big noisy parties, with wine, marijuana, and casual
sex. It was a time of revolving-door relationships, and Clinton pur-
sued a lot of women—including the girlfriends of his friends."[31]

Another friend said that, while in Britain, Clinton had bedded
"a minimum of thirty women—and I stress the word 'minimum.'"[32]
By the time he arrived in New Haven, his sex life was in high gear.
He had to have a woman almost daily. In this respect, he was a
glutton rather than a gourmet. His appetite was so voracious that
any old girl would do, provided she was willing and they could
find a private place.

In fact, sometimes privacy was a secondary consideration. Dolly
Kyle Browning—perhaps Bill's most talkative conquest—tells of

coupling in a friend's backyard and parking in a residential neighborhood, taking off their clothes, and having intercourse twice in the front seat of a Cadillac convertible—with the top down. "He is so arrogant he thinks he'll never be caught," she later explained. "And then there's a part of him that wants to get caught because he thinks he can lie his way out of anything. Usually, he can."[33]

But in the case of Hillary Rodham, it wasn't just another roll in the hay. He found her as intriguing and as inviting as she found him.

Their mutual attraction was both likely and unlikely. In the first place, Hillary was from suburban Illinois and Bill Clinton was from rural Arkansas. The two worlds had little in common—indeed, not even a mutually shared language. The tempo in Chicago was swift, the style abrupt, while Arkansas ran on a low battery and good manners.

The Clintons weren't the textbook definition of white trash, as some commentators have alleged. But they could pass for white trash from time to time—particularly when engaged in Hot Springs-style recreation on Friday and Saturday nights. Bill's stepfather, Roger Clinton, a Buick dealer, was a drunk who physically abused his wife and her two boys, one of them his natural son. He was known among his fellow gamblers as "Dude."

Virginia, Bill's mother, drank heavily herself and loved to gamble as well. The two parents would often make the late-night weekend rounds of the rowdiest establishments Hot Springs had to offer—particularly the dives featuring gambling and country music. A makeup-soaked big-haired woman who loved to have fun, Bill's mother was by no means Junior League material.

In addition to family differences, Bill was not the kind of smooth Ivy League man that Hillary had been dating; and she was unlike any girl Bill had looked at twice. He went for cheerleaders; beauty queens; and young married women with red lips, rouged cheeks, and blonde hair that tumbled in ringlets down their bare backs. Hillary Clinton wore no makeup; didn't bother to shave her legs, wash her hair, much less style it; and barged around in clothes calculated to make her look like a grape picker's daughter.

Yet there were similarities in their backgrounds and personalities that may well have drawn them together.

- Both at an early age lived in awe and fear of their fathers. Hugh Rodham was cold, domineering, and stingy, both with money and with terms of endearment. Roger Clinton was a battering bully.
- Both were close to their mothers.
- Both were extraordinarily intelligent, the brightest kids in the neighborhood, the school, the community.
- Both emerged as leaders early in their lives.
- Both were into student protests and liberal politics.
- Both wanted to transform American society.
- And both were fiercely ambitious.

In addition, he wasn't afraid of her; and she didn't fall into bed the moment he winked and grinned and groped. Each posed a challenge to the other, and out of that challenge came a strong attraction that brought them together, despite enormous and seemingly insurmountable differences.

Hillary was like no other girl Bill had ever known.

So they fell in love at Yale Law School; and, to the surprise of all their friends, they were soon living together. However, that didn't stop him from having sex with Dolly Kyle Browning when Bill was touring with George McGovern during the 1972 presidential campaign.[34]

In fact, during that campaign, Bill—working out of Texas— developed a new technique for seducing a woman: telling her how much he missed Hillary. As one of his fellow McGovern workers, a young woman, explained it: "There is something very seductive about a man who starts behaving like a lovesick puppy. But it's also a challenge." Andersen reports that, "[a]ccording to the volunteer, Bill tearfully explained how much he missed Hillary one evening, then made love to her atop a desk at campaign headquarters."[35] She was by no means the only one. Hillary also showed up in Texas and picked up on Bill's sexual exploits there, already the talk of the campaign organization. Three times campaign workers heard her confronting him with his sins. Finally, she had enough, telling Bill that she would be returning to New Haven, where she would establish separate quarters. Franklin Garcia, a labor leader from San Antonio, ultimately patched up the quarrel.[36]

The couple, still an item, took separate roads—for a while. Hillary went to Washington to work on the team investigating Richard Nixon and Watergate. Bill launched a bid to challenge incumbent Republican John Hammerschmidt for Arkansas' 3rd District congressional seat.

Always the control freak, Hillary attempted to run Bill's campaign from Washington, when she wasn't looking for incriminating evidence against Nixon. According to staff members, she called five and six times a day, barking out orders. One staff member complained: "She was telling us who to hire, what changes had to be made in Bill's schedules, what issues he should be focusing on. We knew Hillary was his girlfriend, but she was behaving more like his wife."[37]

Apparently Hillary also learned that Bill was having a very public affair with an 18-year-old beauty queen who was on his volunteer staff—and that Dolly Kyle Browning was also back in his life and bed. Instead of dumping Bill—as she had already threatened to do—she asked her father and brother Tony to drive down to Arkansas and see what was going on. They arrived unannounced—ostensibly to help on the campaign. They were assigned the job of putting up campaign signs, which they did while gathering intelligence for Hillary. They discovered five women Bill was bedding, and other campaign workers knew of many more.

Clearly, the man had a problem, and one that Hillary recognized. In Indiana, she called up Bill one afternoon and screamed into the phone, "What do you think you are doing to me? To us?" "You know, Bill," she told him, "there's a guy here who has been trying to get me to go to bed with him and that is exactly what I'm going to do."

Bill's response should have given any normal woman pause: "I'm begging you, Hillary," he sobbed, "don't go and do something we'll both be sorry for."[38]

Instead of dumping him, Hillary flew down to be with him in Little Rock for the last days of the campaign. The outcome of their separate endeavors was mixed. Bill lost his congressional race by a narrow margin, and Richard Nixon was forced to resign. Shortly thereafter, Hillary—despite all she knew about his sexual adventurism—came to Fayetteville, took a job teaching at the University of Arkansas law school, and moved in with Bill Clinton.

After seven months of cohabitation, Hillary realized she would have to make a decision—stay in Arkansas and marry this insatiable goat of a man, or use one of her many connections in Washington to find a position with a future. After all, more than one admirer had told her that *she* could one day run for president.

Finally, after a stormier relationship than most, and following Bill's purchase of a modest home on California Street, they were married on October 11, 1975. During the reception, a guest discovered Bill "passionately kissing a young woman and fondling her breasts" in a bathroom.[39]

Marriage changed little about their lives. They continued to live together. She kept her name. He kept climbing into other women's beds.

PART II

Occupied Arkansas

*"I suppose I could have stayed at home and baked
cookies and had teas."*[40]

*"I'm not sitting here, some little woman standing by
her man like Tammy Wynette."*[41]

CHAPTER 2

What's in a Name

In March of 1976, less than five months after the wedding, Bill announced that he was running for attorney general. This time, with the reputation he'd established as a congressional candidate, he was an easy winner. His reputation as a womanizer was also expanding. According to one aide, the AG was engaging in "at least two or three one-night stands a week." In addition, he met two women with whom he would be linked over two decades—Susan McDougal and Gennifer Flowers. Christopher Andersen quotes friends of Bill's as saying that his affair with Susan McDougal—wife of his friend, political advisor, and business partner Jim McDougal—would last for 15 years. In 1977, he met singer-reporter

Gennifer Flowers—with whom, according to Andersen, he had sex for the next 12 years on a "near-weekly basis"—usually at her apartment. Of this affair, Flowers would say, "I cared so much about him. I figured thirty minutes of wonderful was better than a lifetime of mediocre."[42] At the end of 1977, after "thirty minutes of wonderful," she became pregnant and had an abortion.[43]

In 1978, Bill decided to run for governor, and the race attracted swarms of women—volunteers ready to do their bit for Bill Clinton. One of these was a 35-year-old RN named Juanita Hickey, who would soon marry a man named Broaddrick. Her story, kept in secret for 20 years, would one day explode onto the front pages of the nation's newspapers—after the Clintons were ensconced in the White House. (More on the Broaddrick story later.)

During the gubernatorial campaign, Hillary was not an issue. But after he was elected and the Clintons moved into the governor's mansion, the press and public began to scrutinize her more carefully. And they soon discovered she was an unlikely—and unlikable—First Lady of Arkansas.

In the first place, like a growing number of feminists, she refused to take her husband's first name. As she later explained, "I had made speeches in the name of Hillary Rodham. I had taught law under that name. I was, after all, twenty-eight when I was married, and I was fairly well-established."[44]

To many traditionalists—and Arkansas had more than its share—refusing to take your husband's name was a repudiation of the institution of marriage itself, where two people become one flesh, a single "person" in the eyes of the law and the Lord. It smacked of cohabitation rather than holy matrimony. It was also a reproof to her husband—as if becoming a Clinton was somehow demeaning.

The issue had taken a toll on the Clinton family from day one. When Bill told his mother that Hillary wouldn't take his name, she was having breakfast with some friends at the Holiday Inn on the morning of their wedding. She heard the news and immediately burst into tears. Later she would admit she was in "pure shock."

"I had never conceived of such a thing," she said.[45]

In the second place, instead of acting as his hostess and speaking in behalf of highway beautification at ladies' luncheons, Hillary decided to continue her law practice at the Rose Law Firm. "We realized that being a governor's wife could be a full-time job," she explained. "But I need to maintain my interests and my commitments. I need my own identity, too."[46]

Many Arkansans regarded such an attitude as proud and haughty—an excess of ego. Others would become impatient with talk about "commitments" and "identity"—the kind of dialogue they heard on *As the World Turns*. In addition, they would regard her refusal to play the conventional First Lady role as a slap in the face of the people of Arkansas as well as their favorite son.

What's more, because she had stringy brown hair, dressed like a social worker, scorned makeup, wore Ben Franklin glasses, and laced her speech with four-letter words, gossips spread the word that she was a lesbian. Christopher Andersen quotes an Arkansas woman as saying, "Some of the women she was close to were tough-as-nails types. They wore unflattering, boxy business suits, let their hair go gray, and swore like sailors."[47]

Instead of taking this kind of talk seriously, the First Lady of Arkansas dismissed it with a flippant remark, "When I look at what's available in the man department, I'm surprised more women aren't gay."[48]

On the other hand, before Bill's two-year term had expired, the First Lady did something that muted the charges of sexual deviance: She gave birth to a child. Ordinarily motherhood would have acquitted her of all charges in the eyes of traditionalist Arkansas; but instead of staying home and taking care of her daughter, she returned to work at the Rose Law Firm after four months. A number of Arkansans concluded once and for all that she just "wouldn't do."

Both Clintons apparently assumed that Bill would win reelection and gave only half-hearted attention to the 1980 campaign. Neither apparently realized the degree to which Arkansans judged a man's worth by the way he managed his home life. Too many voters believed that Bill Clinton's hardboiled Yankee wife ran both the marriage and Bill Clinton.

Of course, during the campaign, other issues surfaced. Among them, the federal government dumped a boatload of Cuban refugees into Fort Chaffee, Arkansas, and eventually they rioted. Many blamed Clinton for failing to control the situation. Perhaps they saw a relationship between the riots at Fort Chaffee and Hillary's rebellious behavior in the governor's mansion. Whatever their reasoning, thousands of voters turned against the boy governor during the two years he held the office.

So widespread was the defection that in the 1980 election, Republican Frank White scored an upset, beating Bill Clinton by 31,000 votes. Both Clintons were in shock. Election night, everyone was crying, including the boy governor. Bill even gave a teary-eyed speech before a joint session of the legislature in which he said grandiosely, "Remember me as one who reached for all he could for Arkansas."[49]

Bill moped around for months, in a perpetual state of self-pity. He blamed everybody under the sun for his defeat, even himself; and in private he must have blamed Hillary as well. He went up to strangers in restaurants and begged forgiveness for not living up to their expectations. As a lame duck governor, he invited clergymen to the governor's mansion to pray for him (a ploy he would adopt again after Monica Lewinsky became front-page news).[50]

By 1982 Bill had ended his prolonged public sulk. Coddled by Hillary and friend-consultant Betsey Wright, he had finally wiped the tears from his eyes, managed a crooked grin, and begun to practice law with the firm of Wright, Lindsey, and Jennings. He had also announced that he would again be a candidate for governor.

Most of all, he wanted to beat Republican Frank White and avenge the defeat. First, however, he had to win the Democratic nomination. His primary opponents were the current lt. governor and former Congressman Jim Guy Tucker, who was also a loser, having been recently defeated in a bid for the Senate.

But what about the Hillary factor? According to many observers, she had been the chief reason why he'd lost two years earlier. Would she continue to dress like a frump and barge around Arkansas like "SuperMs"?

As soon as the campaign began, Arkansans noticed the dramatic transformation in Hillary Clinton.

- When she went out in public, her hair was washed and even coifed.
- She wore makeup—not the brightest lipstick or the heaviest mascara, but makeup nonetheless, makeup that was noticeable.
- She dressed like a smart southern woman rather than a Yankee lesbian.
- She had traded in the Ben Franklin glasses for contact lenses.

And most important of all, she was now introduced as "Mrs. Bill Clinton." In fact, she was introducing herself that way!

Hillary must have engaged in lengthy self-examination before making this soul-wrenching concession.

On the one hand, as she herself said, keeping her own name was keeping her own identity intact. Hillary Rodham was who she *was*—independent, self-assertive, refreshingly obscene, an in-your-face woman blazing a trail through the harsh and hostile wilderness of a male-dominated society. On the other hand, Hillary Rodham was standing in the way of Bill Clinton's political career. From the beginning, the two of them had set their sights on the presidency. And after Bill's election as Arkansas' youngest governor ever, not to mention the youngest in the nation, that goal seemed within reach. Then, in 1980, Bill was suddenly the youngest has-been in the state's history. Many placed the blame squarely on her.

With the master plan derailed, and faced with the prospect of living out her many remaining years in Arkansas, Hillary had to make a most difficult choice between pride and ambition.

This new Hillary—the "wifey," wearing lipstick and blush, looking up adoringly at her Bill—wasn't a major asset to the campaign; however, she was no longer a liability. Bill knocked Jim Guy Tucker out of the running in the first primary, defeated the lt. governor in the runoff, and overcame Frank White in the general election with 60 percent of the vote.

Though Hillary remained a hard-nosed professional woman and an absentee mother, she had toned down her militancy to the point where she was tolerable to Arkansas. Henceforth, anyone who wished to understand her had to come to terms with the paradoxical nature of her character—and her uncanny willingness to compromise, to back down, to do whatever it took to win.

As for Bill Clinton—in part because of Hillary's sacrifice of herself on the altar of his success—he would remain governor of Arkansas until he was elected president of the United States. And during this period, Bill and Hillary would manage to get themselves into real trouble. . . .

CHAPTER 3

Cattlegate

In 1978—as her husband was on the verge of election as governor of Arkansas—Hillary was dabbling in cattle futures.

At the time, the combined income of the Clintons was around $60,000; so Hillary couldn't risk a lot—a mere $1,000 to dip her toe into an uncertain stream. However, it turned out she was enormously lucky—so lucky, in fact, that a lot of cynics in Arkansas and elsewhere came to believe that luck played little or no role in her success, that she and her financial advisor had engaged in a scam. Her friends defended her with a very weak, "beginner's luck."

The popular media have said comparatively little about Hillary's venture in cattle futures—perhaps because commodities trading is complicated, perhaps because Hillary Clinton is untouchable in their eyes. However, some business publications have examined these transactions in depth and found them highly suspect. Here are the bare facts.

In 1978—when her husband was still attorney general of Arkansas—Hillary Rodham Clinton opened a futures account with Refco, a Chicago-based firm, whose local broker was Robert L. "Red" Bone." She turned the management of this account over to James Blair, counsel for Tyson's Foods Inc., one of the biggest chicken processors in the country and a major Arkansas employer.[51]

Blair's connection with Tyson is by no means irrelevant to a consideration of Hillary's futures account. Over the years, Don Tyson had been a major supporter of Bill Clinton's many political campaigns—according to some, the most generous contributor of all.

Tyson, known in Arkansas as "Big Daddy," probably killed,

gutted, packaged, and shipped more chickens in a day than most chicken farmers and processors saw in a lifetime. An eccentric good ol' boy with a mean streak, he was arguably the biggest chicken merchant in the country, and behaved like it.

A governor could do a lot of favors for an old chicken plucker. And Big Daddy needed all the breaks he could get from friends in high places. For example, in a state-regulated food industry, it made a difference who was inspecting for health hazards and environmental infractions. The right inspector—somebody who understood the troubles chickens could pose and who could use a little extra money "off the books"—might well make the difference in whether or not people nationwide bought Tyson's chicken tenders or Perdue's. So, if you were a chicken man, it was nice to be tight with the governor.

Jim Blair performed a satisfying service for Big Daddy and the governor: He arranged deals that made both men very happy. And it's hard to believe that Hillary's futures account wasn't a part of those mutually beneficial arrangements.

As noted above, her initial investment was small. However, over the next year, Blair wrought miracles that Harry Potter has yet to learn. The account grew like wildfire and stood at almost $100,000 when she collected her winnings. Some of her biggest scores came from selling short—a particularly risky venture because of potential margin calls.[52]

Blair and Bone had an understanding about margin calls—Refco didn't issue them, regardless of the circumstances. "Buying on the margin" means putting up a "down payment" on a contract. You put down 10 percent, say, selling cattle futures short based on the current price. This means you're betting the price will fall. If the price increases, your liability increases and the new 10 percent is higher than the old one. At that point, a brokerage house will usually issue a margin call, asking you to put in more money to cover what looms as a substantial loss.

When it came to margin calls, Bone was defiant—so much so that in 1977 the Chicago Board of Trade had disciplined him and ordered the Refco home office in Chicago to limit his activities, an order Bone didn't follow. He was also reprimanded by the Chicago Mercantile Exchange, which cited "repeated and serious violations of record-keeping functions, order-entry procedures, *margin requirements and hedge procedures*" [emphasis added].[53]

The question of margin calls is relevant here, because had Bone and Blair played by the rules, according to James Glassman of the *New Republic,* in July of 1979 (a publication which, by the way, would *not* be included in any "vast right-wing conspiracy"), Hillary should have received a margin call to put up $117,500. No such call was issued, though it undoubtedly would have come from any other commodities office.[54]

Hillary entered the market on October 11, 1978. On her first ten cattle contracts, she sold short—the most dangerous kind of trading, since you're betting that prices will drop and risking enormous losses if they rise. With Blair handling the account, she bought and sold, either the same day or the next day, and walked off with a profit of $5,300. By October 23, she had made an additional profit of almost $8,000.[55]

Hillary—who had spent most of her life denouncing the greedy predators of Wall Street—enjoyed the exhilaration of making money the easy way. Her account experienced a few downs, but mostly Blair reported lots and lots of ups. In fact, she admitted that while she was in labor with Chelsea, she was worrying about her sugar futures.[56]

Marshall Magazine, a publication of the Marshall School of Business at the University of Southern California, printed a remarkably frank and revealing analysis of these transactions:

These results are quite remarkable. Two-thirds of her
trades showed a profit by the end of the day she made them
and 80 percent were ultimately profitable. Many of her trades
took place at or near the best prices of the day.

Only four explanations can account for these remarkable
results. Blair may have been an exceptionally good trader.
Hillary Clinton may have been exceptionally lucky. Blair may
have been front-running other orders. Or Blair may have
arranged to have a broker fraudulently assign trades to benefit
[Hillary] Clinton's account. Many people familiar with these
markets think that the first two explanations are exceedingly
unlikely. Well-informed traders rarely trade with such
remarkable success and consistency.[57]

In other words, the odds of a trader honestly achieving these
results are simply too high for hard-nosed traders to believe. *The
Journal of Economics and Statistics* placed those odds at 250 million
to one.[58] And the fact that staid academic and professional jour-
nals would state the proposition in such blunt language is an indi-
cation of just how widespread and respectable these suspicions are.
The only question remaining would then be: Which of these two
illegal methods did Blair or the broker use in behalf of Hillary
Clinton?

Marshall Magazine even provides a possible answer to that
question:

Although no evidence of fraudulent trade assignment has
ever surfaced, this method seems most likely to many people.
Here is a simple explanation of how a dishonest broker could
achieve this objective: Execute buy and sell orders in the same
contract. The contract price will eventually go up or go
down. If it goes up, assign the profitable buy trades to the

favored account and assign the losing sell trades to an account owned by the benefactor. If the price falls, assign the profitable sell trades to the favored account and assign the losing buy trades to the benefactor's account.[59]

Marshall Magazine goes so far as to print some speculation on the identity of the benefactor:

> Many of Clinton's political enemies believe that the scheme was designed to surreptitiously transfer an illegal bribe or gratuity to Clinton in exchange for a political favor or for political influence. They believe that Don Tyson—a major supporter of Clinton—was the benefactor.[60]

This series of transactions illustrates several important points about Hillary Clinton and her role in Bill Clinton's rise to power.

First, she clearly believed in the adage that you could sup with the Devil if you used a long-handled spoon. Big Daddy Tyson was everything she'd been taught to despise at Wellesley and Yale—a greedy capitalist who hated labor unions and had no compunction about polluting Mother Earth for financial gain. Yet she allowed Blair, Big Daddy's right-hand man, to manage her financial affairs.

Second, assuming the speculation in *Marshall's Magazine* is correct, she was the conduit for a bribe. If so—and many signs point in that direction—then it's virtually impossible to believe that she entered into this scheme in all innocence.

Third, legal or illegal, this was not a campaign contribution, justifiable in terms of ultimate and noble political ends. This was cash flowing into the Clintons' personal bank account. After all, the Clintons had acquired rich, influential friends; and they needed the funds to travel comfortably in such circles. Ultimately, the cultivation of the moneyed crowd would prove politically advantageous;

but they had to dress in the right clothes and entertain in the right way.

And fourth, the money came to Hillary rather than to the governor—a way to sidestep some of the ethical issues that might have been raised had Bill opened a futures account and beat such incredible odds. In chivalric Arkansas, even a politician's wife is cut some slack. Only in 1994, after Bill was president of the United States, would anyone seriously scrutinize her commodities trading account.

CHAPTER 4

Whitewater

As presidential scandals go, Watergate and Whitewater are different in several ways.

Watergate wasn't about personal gain and Whitewater was. Watergate alienated the president from members of his own party, and Whitewater united the president's party in his defense.

Watergate toppled a president. Whitewater didn't.

Watergate involved a president and his followers. Whitewater involved a president's wife.

But the two are also similar. In both cases the president lied to other government officials and to the American people. Both scandals resulted in serious crimes. Both led to presidential misuse of the FBI. And both were so complicated that the American people have never understood precisely what happened. This terrible complexity allowed the media to manipulate public opinion in both cases—and, to a great extent, to dictate the outcome.

What follows is an attempt to boil Whitewater down to its essence and to define the role that Hillary Clinton played in the sequence of events that might well have cost her husband the presidency. Here, then, is a slightly oversimplified version of how Bill and Hillary Clinton, in an effort to line their pockets, found it necessary to compound their problems with each new agonizing development.

The scandal began in 1978, when Bill and Hillary were having dinner with Jim and Susan McDougal at the Black-Eyed Pea restaurant in Little Rock.[61] Jim McDougal was older than Bill and had been in Arkansas politics longer. He was also a born hustler.

That evening he told Bill and Hillary about "a real sweet real estate deal" that he had found and wanted to share with them.

The "deal" was 250 acres of land on a bluff high above the White River. The scene was breathtaking and the land suitable for subdivision. McDougal believed it would be ideal property for "getaway" cabins and retirement homes. Developers all over the South were making fortunes selling such plots to Yankees who wanted to emigrate, enjoy the milder climate, swim, fish, and generally take life easy. The whole tract could be had for a mere $202,000— And neither couple would have to put up a dime. It could all be done on OPM (other people's money).

Jim McDougal would later recall that Bill Clinton "had no business sense, so he couldn't have cared less." But Hillary—the same Hillary who habitually denounced the insatiable greed of contemporary society—"paid very close attention to the details. She was interested, and she was the one we talked to."[62]

She concluded that what the McDougals said made sense, so the two couples formed the Whitewater Development Corporation, borrowed $20,000 for a down payment from the United National Bank and financed the balance with a loan from Citizens

Bank and Trust of Flippin (from whose president they were buying a portion of the land).

At the time, it looked like a sure thing. However, interest rates soared over the next several years and fewer lots sold than expected. That meant the income from land sales was often insufficient to make the mortgage payments, so somebody had to pony up the difference. That somebody was usually the McDougals, though occasionally the Clintons had to kick in a portion. Over the years these shortfall payments added up to almost $175,000. Of this amount, slightly more than $138,000 had been paid by the McDougals and slightly less than $36,000 had been paid by the Clintons.[63]

In fact, both couples experienced cash flow problems because of Whitewater. The McDougals chose to wheel and deal their way out of trouble. Soon enough they owed so much money that $175,000 was petty cash. Hillary borrowed $30,000 to pump money into the project through the purchase of a house on the property, and then had trouble making the payments. Eventually Bill—by then governor—borrowed $20,000 to help settle Hillary's debt, and the other $10,000 was retired, though no one is quite sure just how.[64] (Probably through the auspices of Jim McDougal, who by then owned the Madison Guaranty Trust [an S&L] and was looking at a nice little bank in another town.)

The story of the McDougals and Madison is itself a parable of high expectations, bad luck, mismanagement, and unscrupulous behavior. Because of all these factors, Madison was soon in deep trouble, teetering on the brink of collapse.

By early April of 1985, Jim McDougal was sure he had figured out a way to save Madison Guaranty from extinction. He would issue preferred stock and use proceeds from the sale of the issue to caulk up the leaks in his S&L.

In order to do that, however, he needed a big favor from his buddy in the governor's mansion. The Arkansas Securities Commission would have to approve the issuance of the stock—and no S&L in history had ever issued preferred stock to recapitalize. Bill Clinton could ensure that approval, and McDougal had every right to expect the governor to come through for him. After all, hadn't the McDougals borne the primary burden of the Whitewater investment?

And he'd done the Clintons another favor—thrown some Madison business to Hillary to help shore up her position at the Rose Law Firm. According to McDougal, the governor had jogged over to McDougal's office, collapsed into a chair, and told McDougal—who watched as sweat poured down Bill's back and onto an expensive blue leather chair—that the partners at Rose were putting pressure on Hillary to bring in more business. McDougal said he would give her some of Madison's business, and Bill bounded out the door, leaving a huge greasy stain on the blue leather.[65]

Hillary and the Rose Law Firm were immediately put on a $2000 monthly retainer.[66]

So the Clintons *owed* them.

Consider, then, the propriety of the following sequence of events, as outlined by Senator Kit Bond of Missouri in a report to the Senate[67]

- On April 3, Jim McDougal hosted a fund-raiser for Governor Bill Clinton in the lobby of Madison Guaranty to pay off a personal loan of $50,000 that Bill had floated to finance his gubernatorial campaign. The event raised $33,000.
- On April 18, McDougal sent a memo to John Latham, president of the bank, in which he said, "I want this preferred stock matter cleared up immediately."
- Around this time, McDougal hired Hillary Clinton as Madison Guaranty's lawyer.

- On April 23, Hillary opened a file named "preferred stock" and billed Madison Guaranty for the time she spent talking to McDougal and Latham on this matter.
- Shortly thereafter—still in the month of April—she called Arkansas Securities Commissioner Beverly Bassett Schaffer about obtaining approval for the preferred stock sale. (Perhaps it's worth noting here that Commissioner Schaffer was appointed to her post by Governor Bill Clinton.)
- Hillary would later say that she didn't remember talking to Schaffer. Schaffer, however, recalled the conversation in minute detail: Hillary had told her "that they had a proposal and what it was about." Schaffer claimed that the call didn't influence her decision on the Madison Guaranty stock issue. However, her assistant, Charles Handley, sent her a memo stating that Madison was on shaky financial ground and advising against approval of the stock venture. Schaffer overruled him.
- Shortly thereafter, Schaffer wrote a letter to "Dear Hillary" in which she announced approval of the stock issue. McDougal forwarded the happy news to Latham, with the following note written across it: "Be sure we keep their $2000 a month retainer paid."

So was that the end of Madison's problems? Unfortunately for McDougal, he couldn't find anyone naive enough to buy his preferred stock.

To save their mortgaged rear ends, Susan took over the management of the McDougal fortunes and bought a huge tract of land that she was certain would solve all their problems—another real estate venture called Castle Grande Estates.

Now, the image one might conjure up of a development named Castle Grande Estates would probably be of two-story brick houses, kidney-shaped swimming pools, four-car garages, bearded oaks, and landscaped lawns—all sitting on a half acre of land, clustered behind a high wall and guarded by a suspicious gatekeeper.

In fact, Castle Grande Estates was a trailer park in the middle of a larger tract of land.

More to the point, it was a scheme to fix everything that was broken and cure everybody's financial ills.

The Castle Grande scheme was a little complicated; but in essence here's how the McDougals, unable to come up with the money any other way, worked the deal.

Madison Guaranty owned a subsidiary investment company called Madison Financial Corporation. The subsidiary company bought for investment the tract of land—and the indulgent parent lent the money for the purchase.

However, Arkansas regulations prohibited an S&L from lending a subsidiary more than 6 percent of its total assets—and the Castle Grande loan exceeded that amount. So they persuaded one Seth Ward (who happened to be Rose Law Firm partner Webster Hubbell's father-in-law) to buy the land for them. Ward received a $300,000 commission for allowing his name to be used.[68]

This arrangement had to be put into legalese, both to cement the deal and to conceal the circumvention of the law.

The legal work for this venture was done by—of course—the Rose Law Firm. The firm's billing lawyer for this project—Hillary Rodham Clinton.

But once again desperate measures failed to resuscitate the patient. Madison Guaranty expired on the gurney, even as the McDougal marriage ended. In mid-September, the story broke in the local papers.

This news probably didn't surprise Hillary. On July 14, more than two months earlier, she had sent a letter to Madison, withdrawing the Rose Law Firm as the S&L's counsel.

In her letter of termination, she wrote, in behalf of the Rose Law Firm, that since Madison "has been relying and continues to rely on a number of other law firms to provide ongoing representation" and that "our representation has been for isolated matters and has not been continuous and significant . . . we do not believe it appropriate for us to take a prepayment of legal fees when there is only one matter we are representing Madison on. . . ."[69]

Then, six months later, she ordered the Rose Law Firm to destroy all her files relevant to Madison Guaranty, including Castle Grande notes and records.

That done, could anyone prove she was involved in the cover-up of Castle Grande's illegal acquisition?

Investigators might be able to prove just that if they could see the billing records of the Rose Law Firm—a set of records separate from Hillary's personal files. But, lo and behold, those records were nowhere to be found. Sought for two years by the courts, with Hillary pleading total ignorance throughout, they magically reappeared later in the presidential residence of the White House. In 1992, when asked for billing records, she had refused to give them. Now she said, "I was delighted when these documents showed up."[70]

Madison Guaranty and the Castle Grande fraud, which cost American taxpayers $4 million, was eventually investigated by three agencies—the Resolution Trust Corporation (RTC), the Federal Home Loan Bank Board (FHLBB), and the Federal Deposit Insurance Corporation (FDIC)— and investigators questioned Hillary about her role in the fraud and deception, even after she was in the White House.

This questioning was particularly important because Hillary had left no paper trail.

She was so evasive and contradictory in her responses that it was impossible for objective observers not to be suspicious. Even some of her natural allies, including newspapers like the *Washington Post*, were skeptical of her sworn testimony, particularly in light of the recovery of the Rose Law Firm billing records in the White House and Hillary's subsequent revision of her story.

The following examples of her evasiveness are not important separately. However, they form a pattern of clever, lawyerly deception that casts considerable doubt on the First Lady's veracity in sworn testimony and raises the very real possibility that even before the 2000 elections, she could be indicted on one or more criminal charges.

When asked about her work for Madison Guaranty, Hillary testified that it was "minimal."[71] She claimed that other associates in the firm had actually done the work. Yet the billing records, when finally discovered, showed that she had billed Madison for about 60 hours of work over a 15-month period at the firm's top rate of $120 per hour.

According to those records, most of the 60 hours were related to Castle Grande Estates.

In her May, 1995 sworn statement to the RTC, Hillary said, "I don't believe I knew anything about any of these real estate parcels and projects."[72] And in a televised interview with Barbara Walters, she said, "Castle Grande was a trailer park on a piece of property that was about a thousand acres big. I never did work for Castle Grande ...The billing records show I did not work for Castle Grande. I did work for something called IDC, which was not related to Castle Grande."[73]

Of course, IDC and Castle Grande were one and the same project, the former containing the latter. David Maraniss and Susan Schmidt of the *Washington Post*—in an excellent in-depth analysis of a highly complicated issue—say of Hillary's claim:

Yet there is evidence that the larger development was commonly referred to as Castle Grande. Minutes of a board meeting at which Madison officers discussed the purchase of the tract of land refer to it in its entirety as Castle Grande. H. Don Denton, a senior loan officer at Madison, said that within 30 days of the purchase, "it was known as Castle Grande by everyone that was involved in it."

Government officials also called it Castle Grande. For example, a Federal Home Loan Bank Board document prepared in 1986 began its overview with this sentence: "The Castle Grande project involves approximately 1,100 acres of land located about ten miles south of Little Rock, Arkansas.[74]

The *Post* article goes on to explain that Hillary might have had a strong motive to lie about her knowledge of Castle Grande: "It has now been established that real fraud was committed here."[75]

Another of Hillary's answers concerning Castle Grande raised eyebrows.

When asked by the inspector general's office of FDIC if she worked on a Castle Grande sewer project, she said she had no knowledge of the matter. However, after making such a statement, when asked specifically about the 30 hours she billed Madison for work on Castle Grande, she replied that an associate, Rick Donovan, had work on two projects for "IDC"—the question of whether or not Madison could sell water and sewer services to nearby properties and whether a microbrewery could be built there, with a "tasting room"—"sewers and brewers," for short.

Later—after the billing records miraculously reappeared—she admitted that her charges to Madison during the 1985-86 period were, in fact, for sewers and brewers. So why did she say earlier that she knew nothing about these projects? Or that someone else had worked on them? It wasn't because of her "confusion" over the identity of Castle Grande, since, in the FDIC hearing, *she was specifically asked about IDC, not Castle Grande.*[76]

When questioning focused on Seth Ward's role in fronting for Castlegate, Hillary said that she had some vague idea about Ward's business dealings with her Rose Law Firm partner Webster Hubbell. However, she didn't mention her own involvement in Castle Grande—a scam for which Ward was fronting as "purchaser." She said she knew Ward chiefly as "Mrs. Susie Hubbell's father."[77]

However, in its report on the investigation of the Rose Law Firm—revised after the billing records magically appeared in the White House—the RTC said: "The new evidence illuminates this period to a considerable extent, revealing that the firm in general and Mrs. Clinton in particular had far more contact with Ward than was previously known."

Later, in an interview with RTC investigators, she would say of Ward:

> "... he was a persistent, demanding client, someone who pushed very hard for lawyers to respond to him, to get his work done, and by this, I mean anything he was involved in, whether it was for the Little Rock Airport or for Madison, someone who wasn't at all shy about showing up at your office unannounced and demanding that you give him the time he wanted right then, no matter what else you were involved in. So he was a client who really required attention whenever he showed up, and that was not infrequently."[78]

And later she would tell the RTC that the billing records "certainly ...[showed] there was a period of time when I had intense contact with Mr. Ward on some matters."[79]

Is she talking about the man she knew chiefly as "Mrs. Susie Hubbell's father"?

The Big Question: Did she know that Ward was a "straw buyer," fronting for McDougal so he could illegally fund his real estate speculation through his own investment company? She denied any knowledge of that deal. After all, she said, her work focused on sewers and brewers.

But she did know that Ward was involved in Castle Grande because she billed Madison for a two-hour conference concerning an option he held to sell back to Madison a plot of 22 acres located in Castle Grande Estates. The amount promised—$400,000. A Madison official later explained that this option, which was never exercised, was a way of giving Ward a golden parachute at a stage when the S&L was in desperate financial shape and about to crash. At the time, the estimated value of the tract of land was $47,000.

Hillary was also the lawyer in another Castle Grande deal, described by Maraniss and Schmidt:

> The billing records also showed that she spent nearly an hour with Ward on February 28, 1986. It was on that day when one of the biggest and most legally problematic deals transpired involving Castle Grande. In a complicated maneuver that day, Jim Guy Tucker, the future governor who was then practicing law, bought the sewer system from Ward for $1.2 million, fully financed by a Madison loan and $150,000 from David Hale of Capital Management Services, Inc. At the same time, Hale netted $500,000 from a Madison loan, which he used to leverage $1.5 million from the Small Business Administration. Of that, he then loaned $300,000 to Susan McDougal. Everyone involved benefited from these loan swaps.[80]

Tucker, Hale, and Susan McDougal were subsequently convicted of criminal acts in connection with this transaction. When asked by RTC lawyers what she discussed with Seth Ward on that day, Hillary replied, "I do not recall what I did on that day."[81] She claimed she didn't know the sewer had been sold. However, she did say that, to the best of her knowledge, their discussion *concerned sewer research.*

She was doing research on the sewer, talking to Ward about it that very day, but didn't know he was selling it? Could anyone realistically believe such a story? Of course, her own records would have shown precisely what she was doing for Seth Ward on February 28, 1986; but, then, she ordered those destroyed.

As already noted, on July 14, 1986, Hillary wrote a letter to Jim McDougal saying they were dropping him as a client. Hillary told the RTC that the Rose bunch dropped Madison Guaranty because the S&L scandal had broken and the firm wanted to represent the U.S. government in S&L cases.

However, the evidence suggests otherwise. Consider the following sequence of events:

In March of 1986, the Federal Home Loan Bank Board began an investigation of Madison Guaranty.

On June 19, federal examiners informed the directors of Madison that the S&L was violating their agreement by making deals without sufficient resources to cover them. In fact, the directors were ordered to come to Dallas and meet with the regional staff of FHLBB. They sent a copy of their letter to Clinton appointee Beverly Bassett Schaffer, Arkansas Securities commissioner.

On July 2, Schaffer sent a copy of the letter to Sam Bratton in Governor Clinton's office. She also sent a covering note: "Sam— Madison Guaranty is in pretty serious trouble. Because of Bill's relationship w/ McDougal, we probably ought to talk about it.

The meeting referred to in the attached letter has been moved up to July 11, 1986, and the FHLBB has asked me to be at the meeting. Please note that while all of the FHLBB restrictions in the letter are serious, #5 and 6 effectively put Madison out of business. Thank you for your support. BB."[82]

On July 14, Betsey Wright, Bill's chief of staff, sent him a memo: "Whitewater stock, McDougal's company, do you still have? Pursuant to Jim's current problems, if so I'm worried about it." Bill wrote back to Betsey Wright: "No, I don't have any more. B."[83]

He was wrong. This is the stock that Hillary refused to let the McDougals reclaim. He and Hillary were still partners with old Jim and his young wife.

It was on July 14, that very same day, that Hillary sent her sayonara letter to Madison.

Noting this remarkable coincidence, RTC lawyers questioned her about how much she knew and when she knew it:

> Q. As of July 14, 1986, had you learned from any source, including your husband, that the federal regulators were about to take action or contemplating action with respect to Madison Guaranty or McDougal?
> A. I do not recall learning that from any source.
> Q. Were you aware that an examination of Madison Financial was underway and had been underway for some months?
> A. I do not recall knowing that.[84]

Note the lawyerly hedge. She did not say she didn't know these things, but only that she didn't *recall* knowing them. That way, if evidence turned up to prove otherwise, she could blame her testimony on a flawed memory.

The odds that Bill didn't tell her about the investigation are almost as great as the odds that she could run a $1000 commodity account into $100,000 in only months. Too much was at stake for both of them. Their Whitewater investment was about to be removed from life support systems. Bill's financial involvement with McDougal could prove politically damaging. And Hillary's work for Madison, McDougal, and Ward could be construed as criminal conspiracy by a hostile agency.

It's difficult to believe that he didn't pick up the phone and call her as soon as Betsey Wright passed him the message—and that she didn't hang up the phone and start dictating the withdrawal letter.

It was two years later, when federal regulators were delving into Madison Guaranty dealings, that Hillary ordered friends at the Rose Law Firm to destroy her Madison files. By then, Ward had filed a lawsuit in an attempt to claim the commissions Madison owed him, so she may well have been motivated by his disturbing presence in court.

The extent of Hillary Clinton's involvement in the McDougals' illicit activities will probably never be known. Jim McDougal died in prison—just one of many, many Clinton enemies who have fortuitously passed away at just the right moment. Susan McDougal, who also went to prison and has since been released, has refused to testify against the First Couple—perhaps preferring continued life to a clear conscience.

The formal probes into Madison and related scams seem to be over—and while Hillary's responses excited some skepticism among investigators, they chose not to recommend criminal prosecution. In fact, in the end, they tended to accept her account of her role in Madison and Castle Grande, despite the contradictions.

Some members of the press continue to monitor the story, to sift through the evidence and to look for more. But by and large, the media have allowed Whitewater to fade away. To revive the issue at this time would surely be viewed as an attempt to taint the First Lady's expected entrance into the New York senatorial race—and who would do such an impolitic thing?

However, one cloud looms in Hillary's sky—at present, a cloud no bigger than a man's hand. The Special Counsel still hasn't issued his final report, and he retains the option to indict her—for perjury, conspiracy to defraud, who knows? Meanwhile, she is parading around, "listening" to New Yorkers, enjoying the greatest popularity boom of her life—and apparently loving every minute of it. However, as of this writing, the much-maligned Kenneth Starr, an honorable and courageous public servant, has just stepped down as Independent Counsel. Robert Ray, a brash young Starr deputy who once served alongside Rudolph Giuliani in the U.S. Attorney's office, has taken the reins, with the benefit of a nearly completed report, and the lack of "baggage" Starr carried as a result of his media vilification. The Tyson's chickens may yet come home to roost.

PART III

Hail to the Chiefs

"If you vote for my husband, you get me; it's a two-for-one blue plate special."[85]

_____

CHAPTER 5

Travelgate

How Bill Clinton won his party's presidential nomination, as well as the general election that followed, is yet one more tale of Hillary's capacity to change her personality and adapt to the political necessities of an America not yet remade in her image.

Following a masterfully run campaign, albeit one plagued by a phenomenon that team Clinton had dubbed "bimbo eruptions," Hillary's long submersion of self in the career of Bill Clinton paid off. Arkansas was a thing of the past. As First Lady of the United States of America, the opportunity had finally come for her to "run something."

When the Clintons entered the White House, it was like Adam and Eve taking their first stroll around the Garden of Eden. All they had to do was name the animals and leave the fruit alone.

But the fruit proved too tempting.

Always the control freak, Hillary noted with displeasure that the White House Travel Office, headed by Billy Dale, wasn't in the so-called "Plum Book"—that is, the job holders there weren't appointed by the president. Like the kitchen staff, they remained as First Families came and went. Indeed, some were lifelong employees with impeccable records. Their job: to make travel arrangements for members of the White House staff—a complicated and important task, one where experience counted.

According to insiders, Hillary said she wanted to put "our people" in the office—and that meant getting rid of existing staff members.[86] So, on May 19, 1993, Dale and six others were summarily fired.

Here again was an example of Hillary's icy disregard for the little people who inhabited her world and got in her way. According to all evidence, the Travel Office had been both loyal and responsive to the new administration. So why get rid of them?

The reason soon became clear: The White House travel business was handed over to another provider, a company co-owned by Harry Thomason and his wife, Linda Bloodworth-Thomason, old Arkansas friends of the Clintons who had moved to Hollywood and become successful TV producers. (It was Thomason who would later coach Bill in his now-famous denial of the Monica Lewinsky affair ("I never had sexual relations with that woman..."). In order to facilitate this removal, Harry Thomason actually accused Travel Office employees of demanding kickbacks, a charge that later proved to be utterly false.

The day the employees were fired, Catherine Cornelius, Bill Clinton's 25-year-old cousin and alleged sometime consort, took over management of the office, though she served in that capacity only a short time.

The question of who actually ordered the firing of Dale and his staff members is still a matter for debate. At first, Hillary said she didn't issue the orders. Clinton aide David Watkins, the man who actually fired the seven, testified under oath that the decision to fire the Travel Office employees was his and his alone.

Watkins would later be fired for commandeering a government helicopter to attend a golfing event—at an expense to taxpayers of $13,000. He should have stayed away from golf courses. Several years later—while playing 18 holes with friends in Nashville—Watkins shot his mouth off and got into more trouble. He told the other members of his foursome that Hillary Clinton had called him and ordered the firings of Dale and the six members of his Travel Office staff. According to witnesses, Watkins said that Hillary's exact words were: "Fire their asses."[87]

Meanwhile, Hillary—whose sworn testimony such an assertion would directly contradict—had begun to weasel. She admitted she *had* expressed "concern" about charges of mismanagement, but she never actually ordered the firings.[88] She speculated that perhaps aides had misinterpreted her comments. "Fire their asses" is certainly a statement open to multiple interpretations.

Watkins' golf-course account directly contradicts Hillary's sworn testimony, as well as his own. However, the earlier testimony and notes of several other White House aides likewise placed Hillary at the center of the firings.

Anyone familiar with her compulsion to control the world around her could have guessed whose story to believe. And few who knew her were surprised at her willingness to bend or break the truth when she was cornered.

She knew she could count on the media to give her sympathetic coverage and to drop the matter as soon as possible. Sure enough, it was apparent shortly after the story broke that it would be buried in the vast and untended graveyard of Democratic scandals.

But the White House wouldn't leave well enough alone. Word

went to the FBI to hand over the files of these employees. Under ordinary circumstances, such a request would have been made through the Justice Department. However, the new imperial White House had no intention of following protocol. White House staff went right to the FBI with its demand. They asked for the files of Dale and the six fired employees; and while they were at it, they ordered up approximately 900 files of key Republicans.

The ensuing investigation resulted in trumped-up charges of embezzlement against Billy Dale. He was eventually tried in federal court and was quickly acquitted by a jury.

However, the high-handed commandeering of FBI files had a much longer shelf life than the Travelgate story. The press—indeed the entire Left—was highly sensitive to privacy issues. What the White House had done smacked of Nixonism and McCarthyism—nasty words amongst the Beltway intelligentsia. And so a new scandal was born—Filegate.

CHAPTER 6

Filegate

Travelgate itself was bad enough—a breach of the rules governing White House hiring and an example of Hillary's willingness to ruin the lives of little people in order to further her own agenda. However, as is often the case, one abuse of power led to another.

As previously mentioned, in 1993—in what can only be described as an attempt to smear Billy Dale and the White House Travel staff and discredit their defense—the White House requested their FBI files. While they were at it, they also asked for the files of a number of political appointees.

White House requests for FBI files on individuals are routine at the beginning of an administration, when the new president is filling positions in the "Plum Book." Usually these file requests are made by the president's chief of staff through the White House counsel and are sent over by the FBI two or three at a time. Such files contain the results of routine background investigations conducted by the Bureau on potential appointees for security purposes.

So what was so unusual about the Clinton White House request?

In the first place, team Clinton requested a boatload of files—at least 900, some say more.

In the second place, the files weren't those of potential Clinton administration appointees. The list included former officials of the Reagan and Bush administrations and Republican Party leaders, as well as other Clinton "enemies." One of the names was Linda Tripp. Another was FBI agent Gary Aldrich. Indeed, the Clintons interrupted their own search for appointees to scrutinize the files of men and women who had served in previous Republican administrations.

In the third place, evidence pointed to the First Lady as the instigator of this attempt to use FBI files for partisan political purposes. In a lawsuit on behalf of the Republicans whose files were taken—a lawsuit naming Hillary as a defendant—the Washington, DC-based legal foundation Judicial Watch announced that it had as evidence:

- "An authentic document and sworn testimony" [showing] Hillary Clinton hired the former bar bouncer Craig Livingstone, the man who helped obtain Republican FBI files. Livingstone boasted

of his access to the White House residence and admitted that
he sought the help of Mrs. Clinton's chief of staff in obtaining
his White House job. Secret Service logs confirm that he fre-
quently visited the White House.[89]

• Linda Tripp testified that the FBI file information was being
  uploaded onto White House computers to be shared with the
  Democratic National Committee—on orders of Hillary Rodham Clinton. According to Mrs. Tripp, Mrs. Clinton "ruled the
  school" at the Clinton White House.[90]

The staff member put in charge of these files was, as previously
mentioned, one Craig Livingstone, a hefty and sullen former bar-
room bouncer reminiscent of the late Chris Farley. In an interesting and highly unusual development, it became clear that no one
bothered to order up a background check on Livingstone. He lit-
erally appeared at the White House one day and took charge of
these highly sensitive personnel files.

Later—after Filegate became a major scandal—a controversy
would arise over who had hired such an ill-qualified hulk in the
first place. An FBI report quotes former White House counsel
Bernard Nussbaum as telling FBI agent Dennis Sculimbrene that
Livingstone's mother was a good friend of Hillary Clinton, and
that she had asked the First Lady to find her son a job. According
to the FBI, then, it was Hillary who brought Livingstone aboard.[91]

Before the scandal had finally vanished from the pages of the
nation's newspapers, Livingstone had been identified as the biggest
political klutz since the Watergate burglars. Suddenly everyone
denied that Hillary Clinton even knew Livingstone or his mother.
In fact, "Mama" signed an affidavit that she certainly didn't know
Hillary. And Nussbaum claimed he never said she did.

Yet the FBI clearly documents that Hillary hired Livingstone.

Indeed, he had been a part of team Clinton for some time. He was an "advance man" for Bill Clinton during the 1992 campaign. As junior members of campaign organizations, advance men arrive in any given location a few days ahead of the candidate, book hotel rooms, set up events, make contact with local supporters, arrange for transportation, and perform a variety of less important tasks. After the election, Livingstone the advance man was suddenly given control of White House security.

When Livingstone was questioned about the matter by the Senate Judiciary Committee, he swore that the files were obtained by mistake,[92] that he didn't know how many his deputy, Anthony Marceca, was receiving.[93]

Mari L. Anderson, who was Craig Livingstone's assistant, told a different story to committee investigators. She said the White House in May of 1993 deliberately went after the FBI background files of Dale and Dale's deputies. Further, as George Archibald reports in *Insight,* she testified in her sworn deposition that both Livingstone and associate Anthony B. Marceca "acquired the FBI files on hundreds of former Republican White House aides after acknowledging to her that there was no official reason to do so."[94]

In addition to the partisan misuse of the FBI—by the way, one of the more serious charges leveled against Richard Nixon—the White House staff violated security procedures in their handling of confidential records. Livingstone's office, where these highly sensitive files were kept, usually remained wide open. The combination of misuse and lax security prompted people in the security community to voice their protest:

> An FBI agent near retirement said: "This is always a difficult assignment. You go out and try to get people to tell you whatever they know or think they know about their neigh-

bors. And you promise them that nobody will ever find out. You know, 'Trust us, we'll protect you.' . . .People are telling us they don't want to talk. You can tell from how they talk, they're nervous. This has had the effect of confirming that what they tell us isn't secret."[95]

And Leon J. Podles, an agent with the Office of Federal Investigation, said the same thing: "It will definitely make it more difficult. If people think the Privacy Act means nothing to the White House—that the government can violate the Privacy Act and use these files for purposes which [they] were not intended—people will be much more reluctant to supply information or allow themselves to be investigated."[96]

Judicial Watch pressed ahead with the $90 million lawsuit on behalf of the Reagan and Bush officials whose FBI files were ordered up by the First Lady, and, since she was a defendant in the suit, Larry Klayman and his *Judicial Watch* attorneys understandably wanted to depose her.

They were stunned when, in July of 1999, she attempted to block such a deposition, arguing, in effect, that she was too busy and important to testify. As her brief put it, "as a general proposition, high-ranking government officials are not subject to depositions." She asked that she be excused so she might "have time to dedicate to the performance of government functions."[97]

In point of fact, she absolutely was *not* a government official. She held no public office and therefore performed no official functions. She was, however, a defendant, and the plaintiffs had every right to depose the defendants.

So Filegate was an attempt to cover up Travelgate, and Hillary's attempt to avoid testifying was an attempt to cover up the truth about Filegate. At this point, even newspapers and columnists sympathetic with Democratic politicians and policies said they were shocked—more so, apparently, than at Bill's later sexual dalliance with Monica Lewinsky.

Yet their criticisms ceased almost as quickly as they began, although the Washington news media beat the war drums for months before the general public finally came to believe that Richard Nixon's conduct following the Watergate break-in was impeachable. As front-page news, Filegate was as short-lived as the World Series. With few exceptions, Hillary Clinton's early abuses of power have been stored away in the attic, like the fading photographs of great-grandparents; and they will probably remain there. Unless, of course, she chooses to run for public office herself and ends up facing an opponent with a modicum of courage.

CHAPTER 7

Vince Foster

Vince Foster was a boyhood friend of Bill Clinton. A graduate of Davidson College and the University of Arkansas law school, he was a member of the Rose Law Firm before Hillary Clinton came to town. He had also held Bill Clinton's first political fundraiser when Bill was running for Congress.

When Hillary married Bill and later joined the Rose Law Firm, Vince was her closest friend. According to Christopher Andersen, after Bill's flagrant and prolific adulteries had driven Hillary to distraction, she and Vince Foster became more than friends.

He quotes one Rose Law Firm secretary as saying that the two had behaved like "two people in love."[98]

L. D. Brown, Larry Patterson, and other state troopers confirmed this view. They said that every time Governor Clinton would leave town, Vince Foster would show up at the mansion "like clockwork" and spend the night with Hillary.[99]

As Brown put it, "Hillary and Vince were *deeply* in love. I saw them, locked in each other's arms, deep-kissing, nuzzling—you have it." They would behave like this at public functions, and even in the car together, when they stopped for a red light.[100]

Patterson described an incident at Hillary's birthday party when their sex play was open and flagrant. The trooper was seated at the bar, removed from the center of the gathering, when Hillary and Carolyn Huber, a female law partner, came there to talk in private. According to Patterson, Vince "came up behind Hillary and squeezed her rear end with both his hands. Then he winked and gave me the 'OK' sign. On the way back, Huber was turned away, and Vince put his hand over one of Hillary's breasts and made the same 'OK' sign to me." Hillary giggled.[101]

Brown told of an evening when the Clintons were out with the Fosters and friends Mike and Beth Coulter: "Vince was squeezing Hillary's behind and kissing her and then winking at me. And right in front of *them,* Bill and Beth had their hands all over each other."[102]

Brown also recalled that, in 1987, Hillary ordered the troopers to drive her and Vince Foster to a mountain resort town where the Rose Law Firm maintained a cabin, where the two would hole up for hours and hours.[103]

Brown said that, in explaining her relationship with Foster, Hillary once told him: "There are some things you have to get outside your marriage that you can't get in it."[104]

When the Clintons went to Washington in 1993, Vince Foster

went with them, perhaps to be Bill's loyal supporter, perhaps to be Hillary's eyes and ears. Both Clintons referred to him as "our Rock of Gibraltar," and Hillary had begged him to come with them to the White House, saying, "We need you, Vince. I need you." Foster, who was making $298,000 at the Rose Law Firm, took a 50 percent cut and moved to Washington, leaving his family behind.[105]

On July 20, 1993, some six months after Bill Clinton's inauguration, Foster was found dead in Fort Marcy Park—a quiet enclave overlooking the Potomac River from the Virginia side—a revolver hanging from his thumb.

Circumstances surrounding Vince Foster's death have never been answered, and a number of observers still believe that, far from committing suicide, he was murdered. Journalist Christopher Ruddy has written a well-documented book[106] and numerous articles exploring this possibility, and the questions he raises are disturbing.

- Why didn't investigators find the bullet that killed Vince Foster? Why wasn't the surrounding vegetation covered with blood? And why wasn't there any bone or tissue to indicate that Foster died in Fort Marcy Park, where his body was found?
- Foster owned two guns in his house, neither one of which had left his house, so who owned the .38 Colt found in his hand and where did it come from?
- Can anyone say for sure that the .38 Colt killed Foster, since no bullet was recovered?
- How did Foster's glasses, with traces of gunpowder found on them, end up 13 feet away from the body?
- How do you explain the fact that three witnesses say Foster's car was not in Fort Marcy Park until long after the time of his death?
- Why did Fairfax Medical Examiner Donald Haut report that

Foster sustained a "mouth to neck" wound, while Northern Virginia Medical Examiner James Beyer, in his autopsy report, said the wound was in the back of the throat and the exit wound in the back of the head?

- What happened to the autopsy x-rays, which disappeared?
- Where was Foster during the 2 to 3 hours between the time of his departure from the White House and the time he died?
- Why was there semen on Foster's shorts?
- Whose blonde to light-brown hair was found on Foster's T-shirt, pants, socks, and shoes?
- Where did the carpet fibers on Foster's jacket, tie, shorts, pants, belt, socks, and shoes come from?
- Why weren't Foster's keys, including his car key, found in his pocket when he was discovered at Fort Marcy Park, and how did they turn up at the morgue?
- Why was the suicide note found in his briefcase torn into 28 pieces, and why didn't it have Foster's fingerprints on it?
- Why should the note be considered valid evidence when three independent experts called it a forgery?

Almost as disturbing as these questions is the certainty that Hillary Clinton was the instigator of a hasty but effective coverup following Foster's death.

She was visiting in Little Rock when Mack McLarty called to tell her the grim news. "It's my fault, all my fault," she kept saying.[107]

Guilty as she may have felt, phone records indicate that she never called Lisa Foster, Vince's widow.

Instead, she placed a number of other, more important calls.

At 10:13, 45 minutes after McLarty's call, she phoned her chief of staff, Maggie Williams. After receiving instructions from Hillary, Williams ran into Foster's office, according to Andersen, "to look for a potentially embarrassing suicide note before police arrived—only to find another White House official, Patsy Thomasson, there on the same sensitive mission."

Later that night, at 11:19, she called Susan Thomases, a New York lawyer, who apparently advised Hillary on legal issues relevant to Foster's death. They talked for 20 minutes. Immediately thereafter, she called McLarty's office. Only after talking to all these advisors did she call Bill Clinton—at 12:56. In bed with another woman in the White House, he nonetheless commiserated with her.[108]

Why was Hillary so anxious to talk to lawyers and staff and so reluctant to talk to Foster's widow or to her own husband?

Simple. She knew that Foster was working on documents relevant to Whitewater, so she might have been trying to cover her own tracks in dispatching Williams and others into Foster's office. Whatever her reasons, after the initial shock, she was cool and calculating in her moves.

Files disappeared. White House staffers gave vague answers and claimed to have forgotten key details. And White House Counsel Bernie Nussbaum claimed attorney-client privilege and scooped up the Foster papers—those that hadn't flown the coop—and cradled them close to his breast.

Then, six days after Foster's body was discovered, a White House assistant found a suicide note—in Foster's briefcase, which had been searched twice before. The note was torn into 28 pieces. It had no fingerprints on it. And some people said it was a forgery.

The message the note contained couldn't have served the Clinton's better: "I made mistakes from ignorance, inexperience and overwork. I did not knowingly violate any law or standard of conduct, including any action in the travel office. There was no intent to benefit any individual or specific group."[109]

He blamed the FBI for lying to Janet Reno, and he also blamed the press "for covering up the illegal benefits they received from the travel staff . . . The public will never believe the innocence of the Clintons or their loyal staff."[110]

As noted, Bill Clinton was so broken up by Foster's death that he spent that night with "an old hippie girlfriend" Marsha Scott. She would later tell a friend: "I spent the night with Bill in his bed. I had his head in my lap and we reminisced all night long. I'm wearing the same clothes as yesterday and I'm going to have to wear them the whole day again."[111]

Later, when she gave sworn testimony to a House committee, she said she remembered going to the White House that night, but that everything else was "a blur." Most of the White House staffers reported the same blur, frustrating investigators attempting to learn the whole truth about the tragedy.

And that's why the death of Vince Foster still hangs over the life of Hillary Clinton like a wet, gray question mark.

CHAPTER 8

Hillarycare

By the time workers were breaking down the chairs after the inauguration ceremony, the new president had appointed his wife to head a task force with the charge of "reforming" the nation's health-care system—the very system that happened to be the envy of the entire world.

In this case, "reform" meant "commandeer," "take over," "capture," "swallow whole." She intended to bring every doctor, nurse, and health-care facility in the United States under the control of the U.S. government and then dictate to the smallest detail how they should practice medicine. It was a task enormous enough to challenge her soaring ambition.

The initial problem she faced in accomplishing this revolution was formidable: *The system didn't need fixing.*

So Hillary and her task force had to create the *illusion* of a problem—a "mirage crisis" in the quality and availability of medical care to the American people. Aware they were adored by the press, Hillary and the president began to refer to an American "health-care crisis" in almost every public statement they made. Bill repeated over and over again that "[our] government will never again be fully solvent until we tackle the health-care crisis." And, during a "children's town meeting" carried on national TV, he told the assembled moppets: "You know that, don't you? A lot of Americans don't have health care."[112]

The message was unmistakable: "Health-care costs too much, and too many people can't get it. What we're proposing is *economical* as well as compassionate and democratic."

Soon, very soon, the press got the message and passed it along to the general public. *Parade,* the widely circulated Sunday supplement, proclaimed in a front-page headline: THE GROWING CRISIS IN HEALTH CARE.[113] And the national news magazines, tipped off that a gargantuan initiative was imminent, picked up the story.

Of course, no such crisis existed. Americans by and large were quite happy with the care they were getting.

As Lawrence Jacobs and Robert Shapiro pointed out shortly after team Clinton began to beat their washtubs: "Surveys over the course of a ten-year period report a stable 84% to 88% of respondents expressing satisfaction with the quality of care received from doctors. . . ."[114]

And over the previous three years, surveys had also indicated that about three-fourths of all Americans were "very satisfied" with the *availability* of health care.

It would be difficult to find a similar level of satisfaction with any other service performed in society, from the cooking of fast-food hamburgers to the repair of lawn mowers.

Yet the propaganda campaign was a roaring success. While Americans were clearly happy with their own health care, suddenly 60 to 70 percent now believed that the system was failing others and needed substantial reform.

Of course, a lot of people didn't have health insurance; however, 64 percent of them were under 40, according to a Frederick/Schneiders poll, and therefore less likely to need it. Besides, as Fred Barnes pointed out in *The American Spectator,* even the uninsured received "high quality health care" by going to hospital emergency rooms.

> Doctors in emergency rooms are specialists. In fact, they have a professional organization, the American College of Emergency Physicians. Its motto is: "Our specialty is devoted to treating everyone in need, no questions asked." Turning away patients isn't an option. Federal law (Section 912) of the Consolidated Omnibus Budget Reconciliation Act of 1985 requires medical screening of everyone requesting care at a hospital emergency room. If treatment is needed, it must be provided. What this adds up to is "universal access" to health care in America, as one head of a hospital board told me.[115]

Barnes's well-argued conclusion: "There is no health-care crisis."

Of course, in one sense team Clinton had it right: With the growing possibility that Hillarycare might actually become law, a health-care crisis had actually developed. The nation was in danger of instituting a system that would put Americans in waiting lines for crucial medical procedures and cost the American tax-payers close to a trillion dollars.

The plan for Hillarycare was drafted in secret meetings over a five-month period. The names of task force members were a secret. Doctors weren't invited to attend. Everyone aboard was paranoid about leaks.

Apparently the final plan was the brain child of Hillary's task force leader, Ira Magaziner—a self-anointed "expert" at just about everything and an old Oxford friend of the president. Magaziner had been credited with transforming Brown University from an educational institution into a politically correct opinion mill. He had also advised General Electric to change the way it made refrig-erators. He was apparently a genius at devising organizational dis-asters, an upper-management klutz with a spotless record for break-ing things that were fixed.

Team Clinton shrewdly described Hillarycare as consisting of a consortium of "managed competition" programs. The phrase sounded wonderfully American. Most Americans favor both competition and management. So how could anybody be opposed to "managed competition"? The trouble was, in Hillarycare there was entirely too much management and no genuine competition.

Without choice in the marketplace, you can't have competition. And had Hillarycare been enacted into law, *Americans would no longer have been able to choose their own doctors and their own type of medical treatment.*

The concept was simple.

- Everyone would have been assigned what was called "a gate-keeper physician," who would have been responsible for "man-aging" all medical problems. (During the debate, the plan was invariably explained in business terms rather than medical terms.)

This "gatekeeper" would have made all final decisions concerning what kind of health care a patient needed—though not in the same way a private doctor would make such a decision. There would have been a couple of big differences.

- Hillarycare would have allotted the "gatekeeper" a set amount of money for each assigned patient's medical care during a given year—say $125 to $150 per month. Out of that sum, the "gatekeeper" would have received $10 to $15 per month for being the personal physician to a number of patients. The rest of the money would have gone into a "reserve account" or "backup fund" that would have been used for any additional care the patient received—specialists, hospitalization, x-rays, laboratory tests, and other services. At the end of the year, the "gatekeeper" would have been paid a kickback out of whatever money was left in the "reserve account"—the more money, the bigger the kickback. In other words, Hillarycare would have forced "gatekeeper" doctors to choose between a patient's health and their own financial welfare.

- To put it in more concrete terms, in Hillarycare, the "gatekeeper" would have decided whether or not a patient would be *allowed* to go to a specialist, undergo expensive therapy, or even have that additional x-ray or laboratory test to determine what's really wrong. And the "gatekeeper" would have made that decision knowing that if the patient's "reserve account" were used up at the end of the year, then pity the poor gatekeeper! No extra money from that patient. No vacation in the south of France. No Mercedes Benz.

So Hillarycare pitted the medical needs of the patient against the financial needs of the doctor—with the only winner being the bureaucracy. In fact, if there was any "competition" present in the proposal, it was between the competing interests of the doctor and the patient.

And there was an additional provision in Hillarycare that was even more disturbing: Once the program went into effect, Americans would no longer have been able to go outside the system—that is, to consult another physician of their own choosing or seek a treatment their "gatekeeper" had ruled out. In fact, under Hillarycare, it would have been a crime to do such a thing—an offense punishable by huge fines and prison sentences, both for the patient and the doctor, even if a patient were willing to pay for additional medical care.

Why, then, did Hillarycare include such a perverse proposal—one that would end forever the right of Americans to choose their own doctors and make decisions about their own treatment? There were at least two reasons.

1. Allowing a patient to pay for outside care would have exposed the weaknesses of the system—the care it couldn't or wouldn't offer to all patients. Some current HMOs have the same policy, and upper management knows that when patients go outside the system, they will discover that other health-care providers *do* more. In other words, if patients were allowed to go to someone other than their assigned Hillarycare doctors for specialized care, they would see the limitations of the care the system was offering. And of course, in reality "doing more" would have cost more. If Hillarycare did more, it would have had to charge more.

2. Allowing people to go outside the system would have given some advantage to people who had more money or worked harder, earned more, and could therefore afford to pay for additional care. For them, Hillarycare would have meant poorer medical treatment and increased risk of serious illness or early death.

Indeed, some people receiving life-sustaining treatment under the current system would probably have been allowed to die under

Hillarycare. While stumping for her proposal, Hillary spoke of an elderly man who had recently undergone successful heart surgery. Such an operation, she said, was a waste of money, a drain on the system. The clear implication—they should have let Grandpa die.

Undoubtedly it would have seemed "wasteful" to a federal bureaucrat administering the Hillarycare budget. But a lot of Americans identified with that elderly man and his family and began wondering if elderly folks were going to be sacrificed so that "gatekeepers" could send their children to summer camp.

After all, Great Britain had a nationalized health-care program; and under the Brit plan, anyone over 55 was denied kidney dialysis. In most cases, that meant emigration or a painful death. At the time Hillarycare was being debated, many senior citizens were receiving this life-preserving treatment; and they were clearly unwilling to die for the "good of the health-care system."

Eliminating full health care for the elderly and for underweight "preemies" would have loomed large in government planning rooms as bureaucrats pondered ways to hold down the cost of Hillarycare to no more than twice the original estimate. This was—and I state this very seriously—the kind of thinking that had gone on a generation earlier in totalitarian regimes like Nazi Germany and Soviet Russia. And it was the kind of thinking that, by the 1990's, had become respectable in the United States—and always, *always* in the name of providing affordable health care for everybody.

Supporters of the program pointed to Canada as a model worthy of emulation. But what kind of health care were Canadians really receiving? The Fraser Institute, in a 1992 study, told the story: Approximately 250,000 patients were awaiting care on any given day. And Edmund F. Haislmaier of the Heritage Foundation reported: "It is not uncommon for patients to wait months or even years for treatments such as cataract operations, hip replacements, tonsillectomies, gallbladder surgery, hysterectomies, heart operations, and major oral surgery."[116]

And what about the cost of the Clinton plan—the real cost, as opposed to Hillary's lowball estimates?

Daniel J. Mitchell—an economist for the Heritage Foundation—estimated that Hillarycare would have "impose[d] the largest tax in American history, exceeding all tax increases in the last thirteen years combined." To arrive at this figure, Mitchell, used "confidential internal Administration documents reveal[ing] that the plan could boost deficits by as much as $810 billion between 1996 and 2000."[117]

And those were only *direct* costs. There were huge hidden costs too. As Mitchell's study revealed: "Independent economists predict widespread job and income losses. According to these economists, the plan will destroy between 1 million and 3 million jobs and lead to lower wages for millions of additional workers."[118]

At the outset, overwhelmed by a TV blitz that depicted U.S. health care in shambles, Congress seemed perilously close to passing Hillarycare or some other universal health-care package. A majority of both houses were apparently willing to support a giant bureaucratic takeover of medical care. It was perhaps the first time in history that the leaders of a nation had revolted against its people.

Fortunately, a coalition of diverse groups and interests formed to fight the Clinton program—and their efforts soon began to make an impact on the thinking of ordinary Americans. I am particularly proud of the effort launched by my organization, the American Conservative Union, in conjunction with Lewis Uhler's National Tax Limitation Committee—more on that later.

Hillarycare was unveiled in September of 1993, eight months after Bill Clinton's inauguration. In July of 1994, a *Time*/CNN survey found that 31 percent believed they would be "worse off" under the Clinton plan, while only 15 percent thought they would be "better off."

In an effort to keep their own party members in line, the Democratic National Committee produced advertisements directed against congressmen and senators who weren't on board. The tactic angered several key figures, including Sen. Bob Kerrey, who told party donors "not to give to the Democratic National Committee."

Hillary was the chief architect of this take-no-prisoners approach to the health-care battle. She went around the country impugning the motives and integrity of those who disagreed with her. The insurance companies were driven by greed, she proclaimed—and so were the doctors. The pharmaceutical companies wanted to protect their obscene profits. She met behind closed doors with figures on Capitol Hill in an effort to whip them back into line. She was Joan of Arc, leading the charge against a wicked enemy.

We at the ACU could stand no more. In addition to publishing extensive briefing books for members of Congress, we teamed up with the National Tax Limitation committee to form "Citizens Against Rationing Health Care," and launched a national bus tour of our own to educate the public about the dangers of this plan. Response was tremendous in city after city. This initiative, combined with the heroic efforts of a wide array of other groups, helped give rise to a full-blown army of citizen opposition to Hillarycare. Shortly thereafter, the plan died a slow and painful death, dealing a devastating blow to the First Lady's ego and to the president's credibility. Hillary blamed groups like the ACU for "not getting it," while admitting that the grassroots assault we launched—involving the bus tour, millions of pieces of ACU mail which told the truth about her plan, and our vigorous lobbying effort in Congress—fell "underneath her radar." The fallout continued when Bill suffered a humiliating defeat on election night in 1994 as Republicans took control of both houses of Congress for the first time in a generation.

Hybris had been punished by Nemesis. She had lost everything—
her ambitious program, her reputation as a winner, her brief but
heady popularity (not to mention her husband's loss of a sympathetic Congress). By then, her "negatives," as the pollsters say, were
higher than those of any other First Lady in history.

CHAPTER 9

Bimbo Eruptions

Hillary Clinton was well aware that Bill spent virtually all his
waking hours preoccupied with sex—plotting whom to bed
next, where to do it, how to keep from getting caught. Given his
documented excesses, it's difficult to see how he performed the
duties of office, both in Arkansas and in Washington.

One thing is certain: Hillary knew he was cheating on her con-
stantly—much more than has been reported—and chose to stay
with him anyway. When the Monica Lewinsky scandal broke, she
recognized immediately the truth of the allegations. Everything
that followed—her categorical statement that the charges were
untrue, her trumpeting of the faith she had in her husband's veracity, the allegations that he was the "victim of a vast right-wing conspiracy"—was no more than strategic misrepresentation to cover
Bill's highly visible tracks.

And while she was striking this pose, the pollsters brought her
heartening news—her "negatives" were melting away like spring
snow. Suddenly, "We liked her ... we *really* liked her...."

This popularity rested in large measure on the perception that
she was genuinely in the dark about the president's behavior with

Monica Lewinsky, and the utterly degenerate nature of that behavior which would later come to light. (After all, isn't the wife the last to know when a husband is cheating?) Since, as research shows, millions of American women have suffered the same humiliation, their hearts went out to Hillary when she "stood by her man." The more she insisted he was being slandered, the higher her ratings climbed.

Suddenly, the nation seemed to forget the mean, ornery, wild-eyed Socialist who had swaggered into town, ready to "run something," to force her agenda on the American people. Scandal had, for the first time, bizarrely transformed her into a tragic figure worthy of, first, pity . . . then admiration.

As previously cited, Hillary was well versed in this routine, having weathered scores of "Bimbo Eruptions" over the years.

As new bimbo eruptions surfaced, team Clinton had become more and more proficient at calmly shooting them down, one at a time.

They'd already discredited Paula Jones by calling her "trailer park trash" and making fun of her looks. She was tacky. She was country. She was Arkansas. She wore too much makeup, and her hair looked like a dime-store Halloween wig. According to reports from inside the White House, Hillary had directed this campaign of vilification. It had her fingerprints all over it—a contempt for people on a "lower evolutionary scale" and a willingness to destroy their lives in order to further her own agenda.

Jay Leno and other comedians had joined in the fun, and Jones's credibility had wilted. When she was finally awarded a substantial settlement—one that contained no admission of guilt—the nation heaved a sigh of relief. For those of us who believe that Bill and Hillary Clinton are basically nothing more than criminals, it is important to note that were it not for Paula Jones, and the president's deception during a deposition for the case, the Lewinsky matter might have never seen the light of day, and Bill Clinton would not have been the second president in history to be impeached by the House of Representatives. Paula, nevertheless, will be known for the rest of her life as the "trailer trash" ceaselessly ridiculed by the president's men. If she received some money, the outcome for her was hardly sufficient vindication, given what she suffered.

Kathleen Willey was a different matter. Beautiful, sophisticated, coolly articulate—she was everything Paula Jones was not. For a few days things looked bad—very bad—for the president. On *60 Minutes* she told of the groping she had received at the hands of the president when she had turned to him for help. After all, she had been an acquaintance of the Clintons and appeared to have no ulterior motive for airing these charges. Even the feminists were briefly thrown into a state of confusion. Then team Clinton saw an opening: Willey had sent fan mail to the president following the incident and had met with publishers to discuss a book.

Immediately, the word was out: Willey had the hots for the president all along, and was only in this current escapade for the money.

The media picked up the cry, and publishers closed ranks and cut off all discussions of a book contract. ("Nothing new there.") Despite Willey's highly credible appearance on *60 Minutes,* the story died a quick death.

Then yet another story erupted—and with an even more chilling tale. Juanita Broaddrick didn't merely claim Clinton had made clumsy advances. She claimed he'd beaten her and raped her in a Little Rock hotel room, while she was attending a nurse's convention and he was running for governor.

She said he invited himself to her hotel room one morning, ostensibly to talk about his campaign and her volunteer efforts in his behalf as a reputable local business owner. But "Billy" soon got down to the real business that brought him there. Within five minutes of entering the room, she said, he grabbed her and began kissing her. Married, with a lover on the side, she wasn't interested in a one-morning stand with Bill Clinton. So she resisted.

According to her account, instead of backing off, he bit her on the lip and held on like a snapping turtle. Then, he raped her. Afterwards, he put on his sunglasses, peered at her swollen and bleeding lip, and said, "You better put some ice on that." Then, he was out of there.[119]

At the time, she told several people about the episode, including Norma Kelsey, a friend who was sharing her hotel room and attending the same conference.

Again, the story was credible, if only because Broaddrick seemed to have nothing to gain from the revelation.

This time, after issuing the usual denials, team Clinton signed off the air and allowed the story to die a natural death, realizing the public and particularly the media were finally so jaded that presidential sex scandals were no longer news—even, apparently, those involving force and brutality. Nervously, the feminists managed to hold the line. The media toyed with the story awhile, then focused on issues deemed more politically satisfying. Within days, the Broaddrick charges had sunk without a trace.

Not long after the Senate had failed to impeach Bill Clinton (following a cowardly sham of a trial), and while the Broaddrick story was hot, Tina Brown interviewed Hillary for the maiden issue of her new venture, *Talk Magazine*. In her widely publicized interview, Brown chose not to raise the Broaddrick charges at all. After all, they were so ...ugly. Besides, the interview was dialogue designed to re-canonize Hillary, not poke the ashes of a sex scandal.

However, Matt Drudge—the Internet reporter who first broke

the Lewinsky story and probably deserves more credit than anyone else for finally breaking the Clintons' lucky streak—interviewed Broaddrick the very night that *Talk* was celebrating the launch of its first issue with a chic party under the Statue of Liberty.

In her interview, Broaddrick told for the first time the story of her encounter with Hillary following the alleged rape.[120]

"It happened at a political rally, in Van Buren, Arkansas in the spring of 1978, at the home of a local dentist.

"She came directly to me as soon as she hit the door. I had been there only a few minutes. I only wanted to make an appearance and leave. She caught me and took my hand and said, 'I am so happy to meet you. I want you to know that we appreciate everything you do for Bill.'"

Needless to say, Broaddrick was taken aback by such a remark. Did Hillary know about the attack, which had taken place only weeks earlier, or was she simply being nice to a staunch supporter?

Broaddrick continued her narrative.

"I started to turn away and she held on to my hand and reiterated her phrase—looking less friendly—and repeated her statement: '*Everything* you do for Bill.' I said nothing. She wasn't letting me get away until she made her point. She talked low, the smile faded on the second thank you. I just released her hand from mine and left the gathering.

"I was in a state of shock . . . nausea went all over me . . .

"You know, I should not have gone to that political gathering, but I think I was in denial at the time. I actually became physically ill. I went outside and told my first husband I had to go home."

In contrast to Hillary, during the brief time they were in the crowded room together, Bill Clinton kept his distance from Broaddrick.

"He never spoke to me or came near me."

Broaddrick also told Drudge that "one of her friends had driven the Clintons to the rally from the airport that day—and the topic of the conversation throughout the ride was Broaddrick!"

Hillary wanted to be sure someone pointed out this woman, wanted to meet her.

"Hillary knew something," Broaddrick told Matt Drudge. "I just don't know what exactly."

Drudge was not the first person in the media Broaddrick talked to about this incident. She told Drudge "that during her controversial January interview with NBC News, two producers refused to continue when the subject of the Hillary encounter was brought up.

"As soon as I told them what happened with Hillary," Broaddrick said, "they stopped rolling the tape and said not to go down that road."

And how did she feel about Hillary now that the rape story was out?

"I'm not frightened of this woman," Broaddrick said. "I am frightened of her power . . . And the spin by the media . . . the way they protect her."

Well she might have been. Had she hauled her alleged rapist into court, her FBI file would have been pulled, feminist leaders would have called her a liar, Hillary would have said she was an agent of Richard Mellon Scaife, and Jay Leno would have begun making jokes about her makeup and her weight. Better to shut up and exit from the stage as quickly as possible.

PART IV

Run, Hillary, Run

"I need this for me."[121]

CHAPTER 10

In a League by Herself

By 1999, Hillary was rehabilitated enough to want to make another go at her desire "to run something." She announced plans to form an exploratory committee to run for veteran Senator Daniel Patrick Moynihan's soon-to-be vacated seat in New York.

Ironically, Hillary owed this unprecedented opportunity in small part to Paula Jones, for reasons previously mentioned, and in large part to Linda Tripp. For if Tripp hadn't taped her conversations with Monica Lewinsky then Bill Clinton's affair with the White House intern would probably never have been exposed. And if Tripp hadn't advised Monica to keep the stained dress, the Clintons would likely have stonewalled their way around the issue, rolling their critics in the process. Simply put, if the whole sordid story hadn't spilled out, the public wouldn't have come to regard Hillary as the wronged wife and showered her with such uncritical sympathy. At the beginning of 1999, a *Newsweek* poll placed her approval rating at 56 percent, with only 26 percent disapproving.

Hillary also owed Rep. Charlie Rangel of New York, who— while attending a Democratic rally with the First Lady—turned to her as the crowd chanted her name and said, "If you run for the Senate, you should run in New York." He pressed her again at the president's State of the Union Address, and she said, "I can't think about it until the impeachment trial is over."[122]

Then, on February 12, 1999, the very day that the Senate failed to remove the president, she had lunch with Harold Ickes to discuss the Senate race.

It's significant to note that Ickes was the first person Hillary called when she was ready to plot campaign strategy. Ickes was a former White House aide who had wielded enormous power until, in 1997, he had been thrown to the wolves when they were snapping at Bill Clinton's heels. Perhaps the best brief description of Ickes was published by the *Village Voice*, another newspaper that can hardly claim membership in the "right-wing conspiracy":

> What's not to admire about a guy who has now officially been investigated more than poverty kingpin Ramon Velez? And like the South Bronx's sleazy Fat Man, Ickes has, so far, escaped unscathed. The resurgence of Ickes (after he was treated to the presidential shiv and hurled overboard) is, of course, driving the GOP nuts, since the former White House aide seemed to be the maypole around which most of the Clinton-gates revolved. While Lani Guinier and other unrepentant lefties sunk like deck chairs, Ickes resurfaced once Hillary began to ramp up for the 2000 race. He clings to grudges, curses up a storm, and practices a brand of brass-knuckle politics that would make his former Teamster clients

blush—the perfect temperament for a New York rumble (you want Nita Lowey watching your back?). In fact, Ickes, unlike the perfidious George Stephanopoulos, offers no apologies for administration excesses like the unsavory campaign fundraising operation. . . .

The very morning after she talked to Ickes, she began making phone calls to key New York Democrats. A week later, she was conferring with Moynihan, who gave her a county-by-county rundown of New York electoral politics and spoke of her "magnificent, young, bright, able, Illinois-Arkansas enthusiasm."[123] (Was he subtly warning her that the carpetbagger issue might loom larger than she realized?)

By March, *Time* was reporting that, according to its latest poll, Hillary would defeat New York Mayor Rudolph Giuliani by 52 percent to 43 percent and would finish in a statistical dead heat with popular Governor George Pataki. The magazine speculated that the talk about her candidacy might simply be a diversionary tactic to focus the public's attention away from the wounded president.[124]

Whoever wrote the story didn't understand Hillary Clinton—her blind ambition, her obsession to run everything and everybody, her passion to use government to impose order and "meaning" on the American people, despite their waning but still active commitment to individual freedom.

By fall, the Hillary train had built up such speed that all the other would-be candidates—Westchester County Congresswoman and longtime heir-apparent Nita Lowey included—had vacated the track and were standing on the right-of-way, caps over their hearts, smiling and waving as the silver engine rounded the bend.

The media were certainly euphoric: Hillary was the most

glamorous candidate in New York since Bobby Kennedy. She was a made-for-TV heroine, a hard-boiled ideologue of the Left who could talk about children and family values—and she would be doing it in what they perceived to be perhaps the most liberal state in the union. In their enthusiasm, however, reporters and commentators ignored some of the problems that a Hillary candidacy would inevitably raise.

First, a newly appointed Independent Counsel was hard at work as the new century dawned; and a number of questions concerning Hillary's role in the various scandals remain unanswered.

Second, Hillary's supporters underestimate the importance of the carpetbagger issue, assuming that, since Bobby Kennedy was able to win a senatorial seat in New York in 1964, Hillary could do the same in 2000.

He made it. Why can't she? Or so the argument goes.

However, a closer look at the Kennedy race suggests that he had a tougher time than people remember. In an article published in the *New York Times*,[125] pollster John Zogby pointed out some danger signs that Hillary supporters were ignoring.

- Kennedy ran less than a year after his brother's assassination— when Camelot still shone brightly in the memory of many voters. When people think of the Clinton legacy, they are less likely to think of a mythical kingdom than a trailer park. The chemistry of Bobby's race is missing here.

- Bobby carried New York City by 711,049 votes, just 8,000 votes fewer than he carried the state. He lost the suburbs and upstate New York by almost 122,000 votes—while Lyndon Johnson carried them. At that time, New York City constituted 42 percent of the state's total vote. Today the city pulls only 27 percent of the vote. So even if Hillary does well in the Big Apple, she will

have more to offset in the rest of the state—which is more conservative and Republican.

- Zogby pointed out that George W. Bush was leading Al Gore
  in his poll by 11 points, while LBJ beat Goldwater by a landslide.
- Zogby asked voters, "What is the No 1 thing you would ask
  (Giuliani/Clinton)if(he/she) were to run for the Senate?" The
  top three questions for Giuliani were: "What would he do about
  health care, education, upstate New York?" The top questions
  for Hillary: "Why is she running in New York? And why did
  she stay with him?"

Zogby's conclusion: "Mrs. Clinton has been a tough campaigner
for three decades and can hold her own. But the bigger question
is whether this state is the right state and the right time. I think
not."

A third looming problem—the residency requirement—has
apparently been settled, but not without a degree of controversy
which may come back to haunt Hillary. According to the U.S. Con-
stitution, if you want to run for the U.S. Senate in a state, you have
to live there. This provision—drafted at a time when Americans
still believed their state was their country—initially seemed a triv-
ial matter to many Hillary supporters and political observers.

To fulfill the residency requirement, many believed she could
merely park a Double-Wide on a lot in the Catskills, stock the 5-
by-5 kitchen with half a dozen pots and pans, put a few cans of
Spaghetti-O's on the shelf, and tell the power company to turn on
the electricity—then fly back to Washington.

Hillary Clinton and her advisers knew better.

In the first place, they couldn't expect the Clinton residence to
escape round-the-clock scrutiny by the same vast right-wing conspiracy that tricked Bill into his affair with Monica Lewinsky.

In the second place—with Clinton credibility already a potential issue for Rudy Giuliani (Hillary had been called a liar almost as often as Bill)—she had to live in a believable house, one a former president and his wife would actually inhabit.

And in the third place, she would have to buy, not rent. Renting smacks of circumvention and suggests a weak commitment, a lack of confidence in the outcome of the election—or in her commitment to actually make the race, should the poll numbers go south.

So the Clintons had to own a substantial house—a showplace of sorts, one they could be expected to inhabit for the rest of their lives, assuming, of course, they would still live together after leaving the White House.

The property they chose was a white-shingled, five-bedroom house in Chappaqua, New York—with a price tag of $1.7 million.

Having lived there for two years (in a rented condo, of course), I am somewhat of an expert on Chappaqua. It is one of those exclusive towns-within-a-town—with a population of 18,000 highly privileged residents, protected from the rest of conservative Westchester County by a towering wall of green—a wall of money— and an incredibly ill-placed population of activist liberals. Only 35 miles north of Manhattan, Chappaqua is, in some ways, as far from the Bronx or Brooklyn as Alpha Centauri—not the neighborhood you'd expect a Democratic candidate for Senate to pick, not someone who hopes to represent the tired, poor, huddled masses, yearning to breathe free.

As president, Bill draws a salary of $200,000. Hillary is an unpaid meddler. And in their latest disclosure report, made public in May of 1999, the Clintons declared assets of slightly more than $1 million. So how could they afford to buy a $1.7 million house? The short answer: They couldn't.[126]

But they did.

The financial maneuvering was intricate and highly suspect. According to the *New York Times*, the Clintons indirectly approached former Treasury Secretary Robert E. Rubin, and former chiefs of staff Erskine B. Bowles and Thomas F "Mack" McLarty III to give them financial assistance, but all three declined. Apparently Bowles said he would, then backed out after the real estate contract had already been signed.[127]

The Clintons then turned to Terry McAuliffe, who was already raising money to cover Bill's legal expenses, the Clinton presidential library, and Hillary's upcoming senatorial race. According to the *Times,* the two personally asked McAuliffe for his help, telling them they intended to put up $350,000 of their own money as a down payment. He in turn deposited $1.35 million in Bankers Trust as collateral, and the Clinton house loan was approved.[128]

However, the deal drew so much criticism from some members of the press and the financial community that the president and First Lady backed away from it, and eventually PNC Mortgage Corporation, the nation's 12th largest home lender, set up a more conventional loan.[129]

The new mortgage was substantial: The Clintons borrowed $1.36 million. Their downpayment was $340,000. The mortgage terms: 30 years at a fixed interest rate of 7.5 percent for 3 years, followed by an annual adjustment to reflect the treasury bill rate plus 2.75 percent. The Clintons had to pay no points.[130] Of this loan, Jim Kennedy, speaking for the White House counsel's office, said, "There is absolutely no suggestion that there is anything improper in this mortgage."

Even experts not known to be Clinton antagonists are raising questions. Mortgage expert and syndicated real estate columnist Kenneth Harney was recently quoted in the *Washington Times* as saying, "Did they get an extraordinarily good deal? No question." Harney points out that the Clintons put less money down than most who take out mortgages of that size, and they did not have to choose between paying "points" (additional fees) up front, and getting a lower interest rate.[131] More will be said and written about this deal if Hillary declares for the Senate.

By end of 1999, the non-campaign "Listening tour" was heating up, and Hillary edged ever closer to the moment when she would have to decide whether or not to be a candidate. While no opposition looms in the Democratic primary, it is clear that, should she choose to run, the general election will be a dogfight of unprecedented dimensions. New York City Mayor Rudy Giuliani—having transformed New York City from a giant crack house into a habitable city—has proven himself to be a giant killer, and Hillary may not even be a giant. While the polls showed her ahead early on, Giuliani is now leading the First Lady, showing particular strength in the vital "upstate" region (which in some areas is more ideologically similar to central Mississippi than Manhattan).

Furthermore, the New York political scene is no place to experiment. Hardball politics was born in the Empire State and lives and breathes there even today. The current crop of statewide Republican and Conservative Party leaders are a smart and tough bunch. They've elected a mayor of New York City—the first in a generation—and a governor. With this prospective candidacy, they smell blood in the water.

Though Hillary would be able to raise all the money she needs, and would draw strong support from the elite liberal salons she yearned for back in Arkansas, she would enter this race at great personal and political peril. A defeat here would make the Hillarycare disaster pale to insignificance, not only in terms of personal damage, but also for the liberal Democratic establishment across the nation. And it would cripple, if not, destroy the future viability of both Clintons when they leave office.

With that in mind, a few pundits, including her old friend Dick Morris, speculate that she will ultimately take a pass and wait for an easier race in a better place, or a plum appointment in a future Democratic administration.

However, her friends and supporters talk of her determination to make this race. Like the nay-sayers, they cite her ego, which they believe will ultimately propel her into the race.

At the year's end, she continued to defy the skeptics by increasing her travel schedule in New York, becoming more and more outspoken on the issues—particularly health care—and appearing more and more self-confident, telling one group of supporters, "Yes, I will run."

The people of New York or the people of the United States may be faced with the prospect of either putting their stamp of approval on the Clintons and ensuring their continued presence on the national scene—including a Hillary race for president in 2004— or else rejecting them and sending them into political oblivion.

That choice will be as important as any other the electorate has made in the second half of the 20th century. This book is offered in the firm belief that the people, when given the facts, will always do the right thing.

Notes

1. John Robert Starr, *Arkansas Democrat-Gazette*, November 27, 1997.
2. *American Spectator*, August, 1992.
3. *CBS This Morning*, April 3, 1992.
4. *Public Welfare*, Winter, 1978.
5. *American Spectator*, August, 1992.
6. Ibid.
7. Christopher Andersen, *Bill and Hillary: The Marriage*, p. 90.
8. Ibid., p. 91.
9. Ibid.
10. Ibid.
11. Ibid., p. 92.
12. Ibid., p. 95.
13. Ibid., p. 94.
14. Ibid., p. 92.
15. Ibid.
16. Ibid., p. 97.
17. Ibid., pp. 95–96.
18. Ibid.
19. Ibid., p. 96.
20. Ibid., p. 99.
21. Confidential telephone interview, November 3, 1999.
22. Andersen, pp. 99, 100.
23. Joyce Milton, *The First Partner*, p. 28.
24. Andersen, p. 99.
25. Barbara Olson, *Hell to Pay*, pp. 42–43.
26. Andersen, p. 103.
27. Ibid., p. 104.
28. Olson, pp. 101–102.
29. Andersen, pp. 104–105.
30. Olson, p. 57.
31. Andersen, p. 81.
32. Ibid., p. 83.
33. Ibid., p. 154.
34. Ibid., p. 120.
35. Ibid., p. 122.
36. Ibid.
37. Ibid., p. 130.
38. Ibid., p. 132.
39. Ibid.
40. *New York Times*, March 17, 1992.
41. *60 Minutes*, January 26, 1992.
42. Ibid., p. 157.
43. Ibid., p. 159.
44. Ibid., p. 173.
45. Ibid., p. 149.
46. Ibid., p. 174.
47. Ibid., p. 173.
48. Ibid.
49. Ibid., p. 180.
50. Ibid., pp. 181–182.
51. James B. Stewart, *Blood Sport*, p. 77.
52. Ibid., pp. 79–81.
53. Ibid., pp. 78–79.
54. Ibid., p. 80.
55. Ibid., p. 79.
56. Ibid., p. 84.
57. "Hillary Clinton's Cattle Futures Trading Profits," *Marshall Magazine*, Winter, 1998, p. 1.
58. Quoted in Andersen, p. 167.
59. *Marshall Magazine*, p. 1.
60. Ibid.
61. Stewart, p. 60.
62. Andersen, p. 165.
63. Stewart, p. 153.
64. Ibid., pp. 99, 101.
65. Ibid., pp. 123–124.

66. Ibid., p. 124.

67. Senator Christopher S. Bond, "Whitewater: What We Now Know," Report to the U.S. Senate, March 29, 1996.

68. Stewart, p. 144.

69. Ibid., pp. 145–146.

70. David Maraniss and Susan Schmidt, "Hillary Clinton and the Whitewater Controversy: A Close-Up," *Washington Post,* June 2, 1996.

71. Ibid.

72. Ibid.

73. Ibid.

74. Ibid.

75. Ibid.

76. Ibid.

77. Ibid.

78. Ibid.

79. Ibid.

80. Ibid.

81. Ibid.

82. Ibid.

83. Ibid.

84. Ibid.

85. *CBS This Morning,* April 3, 1992.

86. Tony Snow, *Detroit News,* November 6, 1995.

87. Matt Drudge, *The Drudge Report,* June 16, 1999.

88. "Whatever It Takes," *Time Daily,* January 16. 1996.

89. "Hillary Goes Under Oath in Filegate With Sworn Declaration Full of Loopholes," Judicial Watch Press Release, July 14, 1999.

90. Ibid.

91. "Who Hired Craig Livingstone?" *Time,* July 27, 1996.

92. George Archibald, "Privacy Rights Deferred at Clinton White House," *Insight,* November 4, 1996.

93. "A Funny Thing Happened . . .," *Time,* July 8, 1996.

94. Archibald.

95. Paul M. Rodriguez, "Clinton File Collections Rattle National Security," *Insight,* July 29, 1996.

96. Ibid.

97. "Hillary Clinton: 'I'm Too Important to Testify,'" Judicial Watch Press Release, July 15, 1999.

98. Andersen, p. 224.

99. Ibid.

100. Ibid.

101. Ibid.

102. Ibid., p. 225.

103. Ibid.

104. Ibid.

105. Ibid., p. 275.

106. Christopher Ruddy, *The Strange Death of Vincent Foster: An Investigation.*

107. Andersen, p. 275.

108. Ibid., pp. 279–281.

109. Ibid., p. 280.

110. Ibid.

111. Ibid., p. 281.

112. Fred Barnes, "What Health-Care Crisis?" *American Spectator,* May, 1993.

113. "The Growing Crisis in Health Care," *Parade,* February 28, 1993.

114. Lawrence Jacobs and Robert Shapiro, in the *Public Perspective,* May/June, 1993.

115. Barnes.

116. Cited in ibid.

117. Daniel J. Mitchell, "The Economic and Budget Impact of the Clinton Health Plan," *The Heritage Foundation,* January 13, 1994.

118. Ibid.

119. Andersen, pp. 162–163.

120. Matt Drudge, *Drudge Report,* August 2, 1999.

121. Mike Barnicle, "It's About Her, Stupid," *New York Daily News,* June 6, 1999.

122. Evan Thomas and Debra Rosenberg, "Hillary's Day in the Sun," *Newsweek,* February 21, 1999.

123. Romesh Ratnesar, "A Race of Her Own," *Time,* March 1, 1999.

124. Ibid.

125. John Zogby, "Wrong Time, Wrong State, *New York Times,* June 2, 1999.

126. Don Van Natta, Jr., "Clintons Said to Have Unsuccessfully Sought House Aid from Ex-Aides," *New York Times,* September 25, 1999.

127. Ibid.

128. Ibid.

129. Anne Gearon, "Clintons Stuck With Hefty Mortgage," Associated Press, November 7, 1999.

130. "Facts About Clintons' Mortgage Deal," Associated Press, November 7, 1999.

131. Kenneth Harney, quoted in "Inside Politics," *Washington Times,* November 9, 1999.

Join ACU Today

Become a member of America's oldest and largest grassroots Conservative organization

- ❑ **$25 Annual** *Membership, Subscriptions to Battle Line, Copy of the ACU Rating of Congress*
- ❑ **$100 Patron** *All of the above, plus special communications and updates from David Keene.*
- ❑ **$1000 Chairman's Club** *All benefits of both packages listed above, plus invitations to Chairman's Club events held around the Country, and Chairman's Club Discounts at CPAC.*

I have enclosed a contribution in the amount of $_____ to help ACU fight on!

NAME _____

ADDRESS _____

_____

CITY, STATE & ZIP_____

_____

PHONE _____

E-MAIL_____

Send to: P.O. Box 96473 • Washington, DC 20090-6473
www.conservative.org

You Can Help Tell America About Hillary Rodham Clinton

This special abridged paperback created for you by The American Conservative Union can have a powerful impact on our country's future—if you and others act soon!

Please consider giving copies to your friends at home and across America, so all Americans can learn the truth about Hillary Clinton.

By distributing as many copies as you can, you will be helping one of the American Conservative Union's most important educational campaigns ever, and you could help change American history.

Please act today!

SPECIAL BULK COPY DISCOUNT SCHEDULE

1 book	$ 3.95	25 books	$35.00	500 books	$375.00
5 books	$12.00	50 books	$65.00	1000 books	$600.00
10 books	$20.00	100 books	$95.00		

All prices include postage and handling.

Mail Marketing　　　　　　　**ORDER TOLL FREE**
P.O. Box 738　　　　　　　　　　800-426-1357
Ottawa, IL 61350

Please send me _____ copies of the paperback edition of *Hillary Rodham Clinton*. Enclosed is my check for $ _____ or please charge my ☐ Mastercard ☐ Visa

No. _____Exp.Date _____

Signature _____

Name _____

Address _____

City _____St. _____ Zip _____

Illinois residents please add 6.5% sales tax. Please allow 2 weeks for delivery.

You Can Help Tell America About Hillary Rodham Clinton

This special abridged paperback created for you by The American Conservative Union can have a powerful impact on our country's future—if you and others act soon!

Please consider giving copies to your friends at home and across America, so all Americans can learn the truth about Hillary Clinton.

By distributing as many copies as you can, you will be helping one of the American Conservative Union's most important educational campaigns ever, and you could help change American history.

Please act today!

SPECIAL BULK COPY DISCOUNT SCHEDULE

1 book $ 3.95	25 books $35.00	500 books $375.00
5 books $12.00	50 books $65.00	1000 books $600.00
10 books $20.00	100 books $95.00	

All prices include postage and handling.

Mail Marketing
P.O. Box 738
Ottawa, IL 61350

ORDER TOLL FREE
800-426-1357

Please send me _____ copies of the paperback edition of *Hillary Rodham Clinton*. Enclosed is my check for $ _____ or please charge my ☐ Mastercard ☐ Visa

No. _____Exp.Date _____

Signature _____

Name _____

Address _____

City _____St. _____ Zip_____

Illinois residents please add 6.5% sales tax. Please allow 2 weeks for delivery.